Bringing Words to Life

Bringing Words to Life
Robust Vocabulary Instruction

Isabel L. Beck
Margaret G. McKeown
Linda Kucan

The Guilford Press
New York / London

© 2002 The Guilford Press
A Division of Guilford Publications, Inc.
72 Spring Street, New York, NY 10012
www.guilford.com

Printed in the United States of America

This book is printed on acid-free paper.

Last digit is print number: 9 8 7 6 5 4 3 2 1

The excerpts on pages 16 and 18 are reprinted from "The Pooka of
Allihies" by Jennifer M. Kohnke. Copyright 2001 by Jennifer M. Kohnke.
Reprinted by permission of *Cricket* magazine.

The excerpt on pages 20–21 is reprinted from "My Father, the
Entomologist" by Andreanna Edwards. Copyright 2001 by Andreanna
Edwards. Reprinted by permission of *Cricket* magazine.

Library of Congress Cataloging-in-Publication Data

Beck, Isabel L.
    Bringing words to life : robust vocabulary instruction / Isabel L.
Beck, Margaret G. McKeown, Linda Kucan.
        p. cm. – (Solving problems in the teaching of literacy)
    Includes bibliographical references and index.
    ISBN 1-57230-753-6 (pbk.)
    1. Vocabulary—Study and teaching.   I. McKeown, Margaret G.
II. Kucan, Linda.   III. Title.   IV. Series

LB1574.5 .B43 2002
428.1′071—dc21
                                                2001055678

About the Authors

Isabel L. Beck, PhD, is Professor of Education in the School of Education and Senior Scientist at the Learning Research and Development Center, both at the University of Pittsburgh.

Margaret G. McKeown, PhD, is a Research Scientist at the Learning Research and Development Center, University of Pittsburgh.

Linda Kucan, PhD, is an Assistant Professor in the Department of Language, Reading, and Exceptionalities in the Reich College of Education at Appalachian State University.

Preface

For each of us authors, our attachment to words is an important driving force in the work represented in this book. Our own engagement with language spurred us to set goals for students that included depth of understanding, facility of use, and eagerness for word opportunities. So we thought it fitting to begin this book by each sharing a chapter from our own "verbal biographies"—our personal history as word learners. The narratives below reveal something about how vocabulary captured our attention and became important in our lives.

Isabel L. Beck

I remember learning the word *earnest*: it was in the fourth grade, and a character had been described as earnest. Miss Cohney, my teacher, talked about what it meant to be earnest and called on us to think of people we knew who were earnest and what they did that made them earnest. Clearly, earnest was a "good" word and the seed to my owning it took root. It impressed me deeply to think about earnest behavior and earnest people. I wanted to be earnest myself.

At about the time I learned about earnest, I began to notice that other people were catching on to it, too. I started noticing the word in newspapers and even overheard it in a conversation. It was amazing to me that I was somehow part of a group of people across the country who had simultaneously discovered the word earnest! That experience was an important milestone in my fascination with vocabulary. What stayed with me forever, however, was the memory that I thought others had learned that word just when I had.

Margaret G. McKeown

Mrs. Cummings, my seventh-grade language arts teacher, took vocabulary learning very seriously. Every week she introduced a set of words and assigned us to write sentences about the words—pretty boring stuff. *But*—the next class would be devoted to sharing the sentences we had concocted, sprinkled liberally with commentary from Mrs. C.

I didn't realize at the time, nor for some time afterward, just how Mrs. C so effectively enhanced our verbal repertoires. But by opening up word learning to group consideration and discussion, she effectively implanted those words and their uses in our growing minds.

And one discussion saved me from an embarrassing misinterpretation. The word was *infatuate*, and from the dictionary I found that it meant "to affect with folly," which I took to refer to joking around and making someone laugh. The boy I sat next to in class did just that—always had something funny to say. So my sentence was "I'm infatuated with Tim Gray." Luckily, before I had a chance to share my sentence with the class, the discussion of the word's meaning led me to realize that it basically meant to have a crush on someone. Whew!

Linda Kucan

I think I was in the fourth grade when my parents gave me a missal, a prayer book in English and Latin. I discovered incredible words in that book, liturgical and biblical words such as *eternal*, *prodigal*, *litany*, and *benediction*. These words were linked to incense and ceremony, Sundays and holy days of obligation. I savored the sound of them in my head. Later, I found the words in books and other contexts, and even heard them in song lyrics and conversation. Always, the words evoked the circumstances in which I first learned them, and I believe they always will.

Isabel Beck's memory shows how word learning can lead to an enhanced awareness of words and their uses in the environment. Sometimes this happens spontaneously, and sometimes it does not. But becoming aware of words in one's larger environment is a very important part of vocabulary learning because it leads to deeper understanding of familiar words that are noticed and learning of additional words. As such, supporting students' word awareness needs to be attended to explicitly and systematically. In this book, word awareness within and beyond school is one of the themes we present.

Margaret McKeown's close encounter with the wrong side of infatuation points out that a little word knowledge may be a dangerous thing. More importantly, it demonstrates the importance of discussing words, talking about their meanings, and sharing reactions in contrast to memorizing definitions. An important theme in this book is our approach to introducing word meaning. In particular we emphasize and demonstrate that dictionary definitions are a very limited form of getting to know a word.

Linda Kucan's fascination with the sound and feel of words in her prayer book brings into play the beauty and power of language. It reminds us that words are the instruments that authors and poets use to enchant us, delight us, sadden us, amaze us. In this book we hope to remind you of the beauty and power of language, and provide a means to convey that beauty and power to your students.

In Chapter 1, we provide a rationale for our approach to vocabulary instruction, which is not a variety of strategies but rather a perspective for thinking about how students learn words and how that learning can be supported and maintained. Among the topics discussed are why direct vocabulary instruction is important, the kinds of word information that can be derived from the context, and what it means to know a word.

Chapter 2 begins with a fundamental question: What words, or what kinds of words, are important to teach? Here we attempt to provide criteria for selecting words for instruction and to illustrate the criteria through a number of examples.

We take a close look at the foundation for all vocabulary instruction—introducing words—in Chapter 3. We raise issues about relying on dictionary definitions and suggest that introducing new vocabulary should be thought about more as explaining a word's meaning than providing a definition for the word.

In Chapter 4, we focus on developing vocabulary for young children. We provide a sequence of activities for introducing sophisticated words to young children and engaging them in interacting with word meanings in ways that help the words become a part of their repertoire.

The focus in Chapter 5 is on developing vocabulary activities for students beyond the primary grades through high school. The following concepts are highlighted: providing rich information about words, frequent opportunities to use and consider the words, and extending attention to words beyond the vocabulary lesson.

In Chapter 6, we focus on teaching students how to make the most of natural contexts in deriving word meanings. Here we begin by acknowledging the unreliable nature of natural contexts for deriving word meaning, but then move to providing an approach that the teacher can use to help students deal with new words in context.

Finally, Chapter 7 presents the concept of a rich verbal environment in which attention to word meanings and uses is an ongoing and delightful aspect of classroom interactions. The chapter provides techniques and resources for creating such an environment for students of all ages.

Perhaps the single most important idea in *Bringing Words to Life: Robust Vocabulary Instruction* is that learning about words in school can be the beginning of students' lifelong fascination with words. Vocabulary instruction that inspires such fascination needs to be robust: vigorous, strong, and powerful in effect. It also needs to be interactive and motivating. Describing such instruction, providing examples, and asking our readers to take a turn in doing the same is what this book is about.

Contents

CHAPTER 1

Rationale for Robust Vocabulary Instruction

As we start this book, we want our readers to call to mind the critical role that vocabulary plays in people's lives and future possibilities. It is clear that a large and rich vocabulary is the hallmark of an educated individual. Indeed, a large vocabulary repertoire facilitates becoming an educated person to the extent that vocabulary knowledge is strongly related to reading proficiency in particular and school achievement in general.

The practical problem is that there are profound differences in vocabulary knowledge among learners from different ability or socioeconomic (SES) groups from toddlers through high school. Consider that—

- First-grade children from higher-SES groups knew about twice as many words as lower SES children (Graves, Brunetti, & Slater, 1982; Graves & Slater, 1987).
- High school seniors near the top of their class knew about four times as many words as their lower-performing classmates (Smith, 1941).
- High-knowledge third graders had vocabularies about equal to lowest-performing 12th graders (Smith, 1941).

Most chilling, however, is the finding that once established, such differences appear difficult to ameliorate (Biemiller, 1999; Hart & Risley,

1995). This is clearly very bad news! But to put it in perspective, we need to consider the present situation of vocabulary instruction in the schools. To sum up that situation—there isn't much. All the available evidence indicates that there is little emphasis on the acquisition of vocabulary in school curricula (Biemiller, 2001; Scott, Jamieson, & Asselin, 1998; Watts, 1995). That may sound like bad news, too, but there is an upside. That is, the fact that early differences in vocabulary remain through the school years is understandable if little is being done to change that situation during the school years. So, perhaps it is not so much the case that those differences cannot be changed, but rather that little has been done to focus on making them change. Thus, taking on the task of providing effective vocabulary instruction is a very high priority for our educational system. And it is our position that the operative principle for the orientation of that instruction is that it be robust—vigorous, strong, and powerful in effect. A robust approach to vocabulary involves directly explaining the meanings of words along with thought-provoking, playful, and interactive follow-up.

The goal of this book is to explain the rationale for robust vocabulary instruction and to provide teachers with examples of such instruction at early, intermediate, and later grades. We can start by describing such robust instruction as instruction that offers rich information about words and their uses, provides frequent and varied opportunities for students to think about and use words, and enhances students' language comprehension and production. But the full meaning of robust vocabulary instruction will emerge throughout the book as we provide examples of such instruction. Many of the examples of instruction that will be discussed in this book were developed for several research studies in which we engaged (e.g., Beck, Perfetti, & McKeown, 1982; McKeown, Beck, Omanson, & Perfetti, 1983; McKeown, Beck, Omanson, & Pople, 1985). The findings of those studies showed that robust instruction was quite effective not only for learning the meanings of words but also for affecting reading comprehension. Thus, it is with confidence that we pass along the details of such instruction to teachers.

Before proceeding to the practicalities of creating instruction, we use this first chapter to present the rationale for the kind of vocabulary instruction that we characterize as robust. Our orientation to the teaching of vocabulary was derived from deep reflection about a number of issues in the field—issues that have resulted in seemingly conflicting information that can be very confusing to those who are looking for direction in teaching.

CONVENTIONAL WISDOM: VOCABULARY IS LEARNED FROM CONTEXT

Conventional wisdom suggests that the major means for developing students' vocabulary should focus on learning words in context. This position is based on three assumptions: First, words are learned from context. Second, school-age youngsters are successfully adding words to their vocabularies. And, third, instruction must focus on learning vocabulary from context because there are just too many words to teach to get the job done through direct instruction. Let us examine each assumption.

Words *Are* Learned from Context, But . . .

It is indeed true that words are learned from context, but in the course of an individual's development the type of context changes. Early learning takes place through oral context, and oral environments play a role forever, but under most conditions they begin to play a lesser role. Most of the words children customarily encounter in oral language beyond their earliest years, both at home and in school, are words that they already know. Thus, the source of later vocabulary learning shifts to written contexts—what children read. The problem is that it is not so easy to learn from written context. Written context lacks many of the features of oral language that support learning new word meanings, such as intonation, body language, and shared physical surroundings. As such, the text is a far less effective vehicle for learning new words than oral language.

In terms of learning new words in the course of reading, research shows that it does occur, but in small increments. That is, by no means will all the unfamiliar words encountered in reading be learned, and those that are learned will require multiple encounters with them before learning is accomplished. Studies estimate that of 100 unfamiliar words met in reading, between 5 and 15 of them will be learned (Nagy, Herman, & Anderson, 1985; Swanborn & de Glopper, 1999). However, in order for any word learning to occur from reading, two conditions need to be met: First, students must read widely enough to encounter a substantial number of unfamiliar words; that means they must read enough text to encounter lots of words and they must read text of sufficient difficulty to include words that are not already familiar. Second, students must have the skills to infer word meaning information from the contexts they read. The problem is that many students in need of vocabulary development do not engage in wide reading, especially of the kinds of books that contain unfamiliar vocabulary, and these students are less able to derive meaningful information from the context (Kucan & Beck, 1996; McKeown, 1985). Thus, calculations of how many words are learned from reading overestimate what occurs for many students.

Another problematic issue about relying on contexts is that many natural contexts are not all that informative for deriving word meanings. This is because an author's purpose is to tell a story or explain a phenomenon, not to convey the meaning of a set of words. Toward getting a handle on the kinds of contexts found in natural texts, a number of years ago we examined the story contexts for several sets of target words (i.e., words that were targeted to be learned from context) in two basal reading programs (Beck, McKeown, & McCaslin, 1983). From our examination of the contexts from which the target words were to be learned, we speculated that their effectiveness in determining word meaning would fall along a continuum. Along the continuum, we identified four kinds of categories of natural contexts. Below is a description of the four categories, including an example of each that was created to typify those found in the basal programs we examined.

At one end of our continuum are **misdirective** contexts, those that rather than revealing the meaning of the target word, seem to direct the student to an incorrect meaning. For example:

> Sandra had won the dance contest, and the audience's cheers brought her to the stage for an encore. "Every step she takes is so perfect and graceful," Ginny said *grudgingly* as she watched Sandra dance.

Here the context would likely lead a reader to ascribe a positive connotation to *grudgingly*. Ginny's comments might encourage one to believe she liked or admired Sandra's dancing. We hasten to point out that contexts such as this are not in themselves wrong, or a misuse of language. The words used communicate the ideas well—*if one knows the meanings of the words*. But such contexts do not make word meaning transparent. The problem is that the situations being illustrated represent initial encounters with these words for young students. Thus, incorrect conclusions about word meaning are likely to be drawn.

Next along the continuum of contexts are **nondirective** contexts, which seem to be of no assistance in directing the reader toward any particular meaning for a word. For example:

> Dan heard the door open and wondered who had arrived. He couldn't make out the voices. Then he recognized the *lumbering* footsteps on the stairs and knew it was Aunt Grace.

In this example, *lumbering* has any number of inferrable connotations: *light, lively, familiar, heavy* would all fit the context, but each would communicate a different meaning.

Further along the continuum we find **general contexts**, which seem to provide enough information for the reader to place the word in a general category. Consider this example:

> Joe and Stan arrived at the party at 7 o'clock. By 9:30, the evening seemed to drag for Stan. But Joe really seemed to be having a good time at the party. "I wish I could be as *gregarious* as he is," thought Stan.

In this passage, it is easy to infer that *gregarious* describes someone who enjoys parties. As such, the passage provides clues to the meaning, although the specific characteristics of the word remain unclear.

Finally, we reach **directive contexts**, which seem likely to lead the student to a specific, correct meaning for a word. For example:

> When the cat pounced on the dog, he leapt up, yelping, and knocked down a shelf of books. The animals ran past Wendy, tripping her. She cried out and fell to the floor. As the noise and confusion mounted, Mother hollered upstairs, "What's all that *commotion*?"

In this example, the reader is led to the meaning of *commotion* through clues from the description of the scene and by a definitional phrase, "noise and confusion." Directive contexts are similar to instructional contexts—contexts that have been especially created to provide enough information to derive meaning—except that the author of an instructional context *intends* to convey the meaning of a specific word, whereas the author of a directive context is simply using the word to get ideas across.

To test the validity of our context categories, we selected two stories from basal programs and categorized the contexts surrounding target words according to our scheme. We then obscured the target words and presented the stories to 13 adults. We chose to use adult subjects because the target words were already part of their vocabulary repertoires and as such would provide a rigorous test for our categories.

The data clearly supported the categorization system. The adults were able to supply an average of 1 out of 13 words we categorized as having directive contexts. Correct identification dropped sharply for the general context category, and it dropped even further for the nondirective category. Only one subject could identify any word in the misdirective category.

This demonstration suggests that it is precarious to believe that naturally occurring contexts are sufficient, or even generally helpful, in providing clues to promote initial acquisition of a word's meaning. Again, it is important to point out that the stories were written by professional authors who use "good" words to communicate. The stories were not developed for teaching the meanings of words.

Given the issues discussed above, it must be acknowledged that relying on wide reading for vocabulary growth adds to the inequities in individual differences in vocabulary knowledge. Struggling readers do not read well enough to make wide reading an option. To acquire word knowledge from reading requires adequate decoding skills, the ability to recognize that a word is unknown, and the competency of being able to extract meaningful information about the word from the context. Readers cannot be engaging with the latter two if they are struggling with decoding. Thus, depending on wide reading as a source of vocabulary growth leaves those children and young people who are most in need of enhancing their vocabulary repertoires with a very serious deficit.

▪ *You Try It* ▪

Choose an excerpt from a magazine article, newspaper, or novel. Select 10 target words and categorize them as having one of the following contexts: **misdirective, nondirective, general**, or **directive**. Make a photocopy of the excerpt and block out the 10 target words. Ask a few adults to try to figure out what the missing words are. Words in what kinds of contexts were most difficult for readers to figure out? Which were easiest? Do your results agree with ours?

School-Age Children *Are* Learning Words, But . . .

The second assumption we noted as justification for an emphasis on learning from context comes from the notion that school-age children are successfully learning words. The implication follows that since students are learning words, we don't need to worry too much about directly adding words to their vocabularies. Supporting this notion are numbers that are bandied around about how many words a day students learn. Specific estimates of vocabulary growth vary widely, from 3 (Joos, 1964) to 20 new words a day (Miller, 1978). A figure of 7 words per day is probably the most commonly cited. Even if these numbers are accurate, they are averages and thus do not represent all children and especially do not represent those who are at-risk, struggling, and lower achievers. Although it may be the case that *some* students are learning as many as 7 new words a day, many others may be learning only 1 or 2, or indeed not any at all.

There *Are* Too Many Words to Teach, But . . .

Finally, the major argument for emphasizing learning from context comes from those who have examined the number of words that students will encounter during their school years and pronounced the task of directly teaching vocabulary simply too large. The logic that follows is that there is virtually no choice but to emphasize learning from context. A major point that we will emphasize, however, is that not *all* words call for attention. It is this situation that makes direct instruction in word meanings feasible, for if all words in the language required instruction equally, clearly there would be too many words to cover in school.

To get a perspective on the kinds of words that need instructional attention, consider a mature literate individual's vocabulary as comprising three tiers (Beck & McKeown, 1985). The first tier consists of the most basic words—*clock, baby, happy, walk*, and so on. Words in this tier rarely require instructional attention to their meanings in school. The third tier is made up of words whose frequency of use is quite low and often limited to specific domains. Some examples might be *isotope, lathe, peninsula*, and *refinery*. In general, a rich understanding of these words would not be of high utility for most learners. These words are probably best learned when a specific need arises, such as introducing *peninsula* during a geography lesson.

The second tier contains words that are of high frequency for mature language users and are found across a variety of domains. Examples include *coincidence, absurd, industrious*, and *fortunate*. Because of the large role they play in a language user's repertoire, rich knowledge of words in the second tier can have a powerful impact on verbal functioning. Thus, instruction directed toward Tier Two words can be most productive.

How large is the task of teaching Tier Two words? We can get a handle on the size of the effort required by extrapolating from Nagy and Anderson's (1984) analysis of words in printed school English for third through ninth grade. Nagy and Anderson estimate that good readers in this age range read approximately 1 million words of text per year. They organized these words into word families, or groups of related words such as *introduce, introduction, reintroduce*, and *introducing*, and further estimate that half of the 88,500 word families they calculate to exist in printed school English are so rare that even avid readers may encounter them only once in their lifetime of reading. Using these figures, it seems reasonable to consider word families that would be encountered at least once every 10 years as comprising Tiers One and Two. These are words that occur once or more in 10 million running words of text. Our best estimate of Tier One, the most familiar words that need no instruction, is 8,000 word families. We base this number on Nagy and Anderson's statement that a typical third grader likely knows about 8,000 words. That leaves about 7,000 word families for Tier Two.

Seven thousand words may still seem like quite a large number for instruction to undertake over the course of, say, kindergarten through ninth grade. That would amount to an average of 700 words per year. So, would a reasonable goal be to teach them all?—Or teach half of them? There is no way to answer that question with certainty. But we assert that attention to a substantial portion of those words, say, an average of 400 per year, would make a significant contribution to an individual's verbal functioning. Aiming for this number of words would allow the depth of instruction needed to affect students' text comprehension ability. We believe this to be the case because about 400 words per year conforms to the rate at which we taught words in our previous research, which resulted in improvements in word knowledge and in comprehension of texts containing the instructed words (Beck et al., 1982).

In summary, written context is clearly an important source of new vocabulary for any reader. But relying on learning word meanings from independent reading is not an adequate way to deal with students' vocabulary development.

WHAT DOES IT MEAN TO KNOW A WORD?

Another point of confusion affecting decisions about how to promote students' vocabulary development is the issue of what exactly does it mean to know a word? Simply put, knowing a word is not an all-or-nothing proposition: It is not the case that one either knows or does not know a word. In fact, word knowledge is a rather complex concept. We will focus on two of the complexities here. The first is that the extent of knowledge one may have about individual words can range from a little to a lot, and the second is that there are qualitatively different kinds of knowledge about words.

One of the simplest notions about word knowledge is Carey's (1978) distinction between what she called fast mapping and extended mapping to describe how young learners can very quickly get a sense of a word's meaning (fast mapping). But full understanding and use (extended mapping) occurs only over time and multiple encounters.

Dale (1965) offered a description of the extent of word knowledge in terms of four stages:

- Stage 1: Never saw it before.
- Stage 2: Heard it, but doesn't know what it means.

- Stage 3: Recognizes it in context as having something to do with
  _____.
- Stage 4: Knows it well.

In earlier work (Beck, McKeown, & Omanson, 1987), we suggested that an individual's knowledge about a word can also be described as falling along a continuum. We suggested the following points on such a continuum:

- No knowledge.
- General sense, such as knowing *mendacious* has a negative connotation.
- Narrow, context-bound knowledge, such as knowing that a *radiant* bride is a beautifully smiling happy one, but unable to describe an individual in a different context as radiant.
- Having knowledge of a word but not being able to recall it readily enough to use it in appropriate situations.
- Rich, decontextualized knowledge of a word's meaning, its relationship to other words, and its extension to metaphorical uses, such as understanding what someone is doing when they are *devouring* a book.

Another aspect of word knowledge is its qualitative dimensions— the kind of knowledge one has about a word and the uses to which that knowledge can be put. Probably the earliest such description is Cronbach's (1942). The dimensions he discussed were as follows:

- *Generalization*: The ability to define a word.
- *Application*: The ability to select or recognize situations appropriate to a word.
- *Breadth*: Knowledge of multiple meanings.
- *Precision*: The ability to apply a term correctly to all situations and to recognize inappropriate use.
- *Availability*: The actual use of a word in thinking and discourse.

Calfee and Drum (1986) offer a description that covers much the same territory as that of Cronbach, but theirs includes some additional dimensions such as facile access and appreciation of metaphor, analogy, and wordplay. Kameenui, Dixon, and Carnine's (1987) discussion of dimensions of knowledge adds an interesting facet, which they labeled "derived knowledge." That is, an individual may derive enough information about a word to understand it in the context being read or heard, but then not remember the information, and thus does not "learn" the word.

Miller's (1978) description of dimensions of word knowledge adds the important consideration of the relationship of a word to other concepts, such as topics to which the word can apply and the kinds of discourse in which the word is typically found. The importance of the relationship to other words is illustrated well in two examples described by Nagy and Scott (2000): "How well a person knows the meaning of *whale* depends in part on their understanding of *mammal*. A person who already knows the words *hot*, *cold*, and *cool* has already acquired some of the components of the word *warm*, even if the word *warm* has not yet been encountered" (p. 272; italic in their original).

Further dimensions of word knowledge include its register, that is, whether a word is used in formal or less formal contexts, its grammatical form, and its affective connotations (Nagy & Scott, 2000). And, as if all of the above were not complicated enough, Nagy and Scott point out that different facets of word knowledge are relatively independent. Thus, a learner might know the definition of a word but be unable to produce a context for it, or be able to use it in seemingly appropriate ways but actually have a misunderstanding of its meaning.

What it means to know a word is clearly a complicated, multifaceted matter, and one that has serious implications for how words are taught and how word knowledge is measured. For example, how do you decide whether instruction is adequate for students to learn the words? That depends on what kind of learning is desired. We think that most often the goal that teachers have is for the students to be able to use the instructed words in understanding a text containing those words and to recall the words well enough to use them in speech or writing. That calls for a deep kind of knowledge.

And how do we measure whether knowledge has been attained? If the goal is for students to fully understand and use words, then evaluations based on simple synonym matching or multiple-choice definitions will not tell us if that goal has been reached. Those kinds of measures cannot differentiate shallow from deep word knowledge.

The multifaceted nature of word knowledge also has implications for the knowledge base on vocabulary learning. That is, answers to questions about how words are learned, the number of words students know, and the effects of various kinds of instruction must be interpreted in light of the kind of evidence for "knowing a word" that underlies those answers. For instance, measures of superficial knowledge may overestimate how many words a person knows usefully.

▪ *You Try It* ▪

Completing the accompanying chart should provide some evidence for the notion that word knowledge is indeed multifaceted. Put a check under the appropriate category to show your knowledge of each word.

Word	Know it well, can explain it, use it	Know something about it, can relate it to a situation	Have seen or heard the word	Do not know the word
tyranny				
surreptitious				
grapnel				
purport				
sensitive				
dubious				

MAKING VOCABULARY INSTRUCTION COME TO LIFE

People who have large vocabularies tend to be intrigued with words. As such, a major impetus for writing this book is our concern that school vocabulary instruction tends to be dull, rather than of the sort that might instigate student's interest and awareness of words. Becoming interested and aware of words is not a likely outcome from the way instruction is typically handled, which is to have students look up definitions in a dictionary or glossary (Scott et al., 1998; Watts, 1995). Indeed, asking students to look up words in the dictionary and use them in a sentence is a stereotypical example of what students find uninteresting in school.

Less than interesting instruction is not a problem merely because we want students to enjoy classroom activities. Rather, students need to develop an interest and awareness in words beyond vocabulary school assignments in order to adequately build their vocabulary repertoires. Among what needs to occur is that students need to keep using words if they are to "own" new words. Students need to notice words in their environments whose meanings they do not know. They need to become aware of and explore relationships among words in order to refine and fully develop word meanings. Indeed, being curious about the meaning of an unknown word that one encounters and about how it relates to other words is a hallmark of those who develop large vocabularies.

Development of these facets of word learning cannot just rely on students spontaneously engaging with words on their own, as it simply will not occur in many cases. Rather, these facets must be the direct focus of instructional conditions. It has been our experience that students become interested and enthusiastic about words when instruction is rich and lively, and that conditions can be arranged that encourage them to notice words in environments beyond school.

We have developed such instructional activities and procedures for research, but we have only described them generally, as was needed to report on the studies in academic journals. However, we have shared these techniques with a number of teachers who virtually *always* report what a difference they make in terms of students' interest in vocabulary. The teachers sent us anecdote after anecdote of students' enthusiasm and involvement with words. Their experiences have reminded us of what we saw in classrooms in the 1980s when we implemented our vocabulary instruction materials for research purposes.

Let us tell you of some that we remember from our early vocabulary studies. The first is from an activity in which we asked students to make decisions about words that could belong together and why they could. One student perplexed us with his choice of *eavesdrop* and *gregarious*. When asked why they went together, he responded, "If someone reports you to the teacher for talking to a friend, they are eavesdropping and you're being gregarious." This kind of ability to make an unusual but very fitting relationship illustrates the depth of understanding that had developed from the kind of instruction he had experienced. Our strong hunch is that these words will be available to him in all facets of literacy.

During school assemblies, a rumble would go through the place in the auditorium where the class in which we had implemented our vocabulary approach was sitting when a speaker mentioned one of the words they had learned. Some examples include when a newspaper reporter was introduced as a *journalist*, when the principal asked particular students to stand to be *commended* for some accomplishment, in a safety discussion when the crossing guard told the students they shouldn't be *meandering* across the street. At first, the principal and some of the other teachers were a little disturbed about the behavior of the class, but when they found out that the reason behind it was the students' excitement in learning new words, they were impressed. In fact, the art teacher got a copy of the word list and began sprinkling the words into her conversations with the target class, and she was delighted with the results.

Very recently, we drew on our earlier experiences with vocabulary instruction for students in the intermediate grades to create instruction for children in the earliest grades that introduced sophisticated words to the children and developed their ability to use the words. The new vocabulary work was done under a larger research and development project, which we call Text Talk (Beck & McKeown, 2001; McKeown & Beck, in press), and will describe in Chapter 4. The teachers who implemented the Text Talk vocabulary instruction reported the children's excitement with vocabulary. And we saw it again for ourselves in our new work. Our favorite recent anecdote is about the first grader who reported to his teacher, "I told my mother that I was going to act more *mature*, and she took me to Toys R Us."

Our goal in this book is to support teachers in their development of vocabulary instruction that is targeted to getting the kinds of effects captured in the anecdotes. We hope that the pages that follow enable teachers to build the understanding, the motivation, and the resources to do that.

CHAPTER 2

Choosing Words to Teach

The teacher's edition for a fourth-grade anthology suggests teaching the following words before inviting students to read an excerpt from *Charlotte's Web* (White, 1952): *comfort, cunning, endure, friendless, frolic, lonely, soaked,* and *stealthily.* Why do you think these words were selected? One obvious reason for selecting words to teach is that students do not know the words. Although *cunning, endure, frolic,* and *stealthily* are probably unfamiliar to most fourth graders, *comfort, friendless, lonely,* and *soaked* are probably not. Familiarity does not seem to be the principle used to make the selection. What about importance or usefulness? Are the selected words useful for writing or talking? Would the words be important to know because they appear in other texts with a high degree of frequency? Some—but not all—of the words might be considered useful or important. Thus, the question remains: Why were the words selected? The purpose of this chapter is to consider what principles might be used for selecting words to teach.

USEFUL WORDS

As a way to begin thinking about which words to teach, consider that words in the language have different levels of utility. In this regard, we have found our notion of tiers, as discussed in Chapter 1, to be one helpful lens through which to consider words for instructional attention. Recall that Tier One consists of the most basic words—*clock, baby, happy*—rarely requiring instruction in school. Tier Three includes words whose frequency of use is quite low, often being limited to specific domains—*isotope, lathe, peninsula*—and probably best learned when needed in a content area. Tier Two words are high-frequency words for mature language users—*coincidence, absurd, industrious*—and thus instruction in these words can add productively to an individual's language ability.

IDENTIFYING TIER TWO WORDS IN TEXTS

To get an idea of the process of identifying Tier Two words, consider an example. Below is the opening paragraph of a retelling of an old tale (Kohnke, 2001, p. 12) about a donkey who is under a magical spell that forces him to do the chores for a group of lazy servants. The story would likely be of interest to third and fourth graders.

> *Johnny Harrington was a kind master who treated his servants fairly. He was also a successful wool <u>merchant</u>, and his business <u>required</u> that he travel often. In his absence, his servants would <u>tend</u> to the fields and cattle and <u>maintain</u> the upkeep of his mansion. They <u>performed</u> their duties happily, for they felt <u>fortunate</u> to have such a <u>benevolent</u> and trusting master.*

The underlined words are those we identified as consistent with the notion of Tier Two words. That is, most of the words are likely to appear frequently in a wide variety of texts and in the written and oral language of mature language users. (Note: We chose this paragraph because there were so many candidate Tier Two words; however, most grade-level material would not have so many words in only one paragraph.)

One "test" of whether a word meets the Tier Two criterion of being a useful addition to students' repertoires is to think about whether the students already have ways to express the concepts represented by the words. Would students be able to explain these words using words that are already well known to them? If that is the case, it suggests that the new words offer students more precise or mature ways of referring to ideas they already know about. One way to answer the question is to think about how average third and fourth graders would talk about the concepts represented by the Tier Two words. We think that students would be likely to offer the explanations shown in the accompanying list.

Tier Two words	Students' likely expressions
merchant	salesperson or clerk
required	have to
tend	take care of
maintain	keep going
performed	did
fortunate	lucky
benevolent	kind

Adding the seven target words to young students' vocabulary repertoires would seem to be quite productive, because learning the words would allow students to describe with greater specificity people and situations with which they already have some familiarity. Note that these words are not simple synonyms of the familiar ones, however, instead representing more precise or more complex forms of the familiar words. *Maintain* means not only "keep going," for example, but also "to continue something in its present condition or at its present level." *Benevolent* has the dimension of tolerance as well as kindness.

SELECTING FROM A POOL OF WORDS

The decision about which words to teach must also take into account how many words to teach in conjunction with any given text or lesson. Given that students are learning vocabulary in social studies and science as well as reading or language arts, there needs to be some basis for limiting the number of words so that students will have the opportunity to learn some words well.

Now consider which of the words will be most useful in helping students understand the above paragraph. For the seven words noted there, our thinking is that *fortunate* is particularly important because the fact that the servants thought they were lucky is an important condition of the story. Similarly, *benevolent* plays an important role in setting up the story, as the servants appreciate their master's kindness and do not want

to upset their pleasant living situation. If one other word were to be selected, a good choice would be *merchant*. *Merchant* is a word that comes
up in fourth- and fifth-grade social studies textbooks in discussions of
colonization of the Americas (e.g., "European *merchants* were eager to
locate new resources like tobacco and indigo which could be found in
the colonies"; or "Colonial *merchants* were dismayed by the taxes on
English goods which meant higher prices for their customers but no
more profit for themselves").

The other candidate words, *tend, required, performed,* and *maintain,* are also words of strong general utility, and the choice of whether to
include any more words is based solely on considering how many words
one thinks students can usefully handle.

▪ *You Try It* ▪

Below is another excerpt from the tale about the donkey under
the magical spell described above (Kohnke, 2001, p. 12). You
might find it useful to try your hand at identifying Tier Two
words. You will get to see our choices below the excerpt, so that
you can compare your selections with ours.

> *The servants would never comment on this strange occurrence
> [finding the kitchen clean even though none of them were seen
> doing the cleaning], each servant hoping the other had tended to
> the chores. Never would they mention the loud noises they'd
> hear emerging from the kitchen in the in middle of the night. Nor
> would they admit to pulling the covers under their chins as they
> listened to the sound of haunting laughter that drifted down
> the halls to their bedrooms each night. In reality, they knew
> there was a more sinister reason behind their good fortune.*

Which words did you select? Trying to be all-inclusive, selecting
any words that might fit Tier Two, we chose *comment, occurrence,
tended, mention, emerging, admit, haunting, reality, sinister,* and *fortune*.
We considered them Tier Two words as we viewed them as fairly "general but sophisticated words." That is, they are not the most basic or
common ways of expressing ideas, but they are familiar to mature language users as ordinary as opposed to specialized language. The con-

cepts embodied in each word are ones that students already have some understanding of, as shown in the accompanying list.

Tier Two words	Students' likely expressions
comment	something someone has to say
occurrence	something happening
tended	took care of
mention	tell
emerging	coming out
admit	to say you did something
haunting	scary
reality	being read
sinister	scary
fortune	luck

Now, the notion of tiers of words is not a precise one, and the lines between tiers are not clear-cut, so your selection may not match ours. Thinking in terms of tiers is just a starting point—a way of framing the task of choosing candidate words for instruction (see the accompanying box). Even within Tier Two, some words will be more easily familiar and some will be more useful than others. For example, our hunch is that *admit, reality*, and *fortune* are likely known to most fourth or fifth graders; that *tended* is not often used in a way that is key to understanding; and that fifth graders may already associate *haunting* with scary things—a Halloween context—

Some Criteria for Identifying Tier Two Words

- *Importance and utility*: Words that are characteristic of mature language users and appear frequently across a variety of domains.
- *Instructional potential*: Words that can be worked with in a variety of ways so that students can build rich representations of them and of their connections to other words and concepts.
- *Conceptual understanding*: Words for which students understand the general concept but provide precision and specificity in describing the concept.

which is fitting for this story. Thus we ended up with *comment, occurrence, mention, emerging,* and *sinister.* We judged the first four of these to be most useful across a range of contexts, and we chose *sinister* because it is a strong word with emotional impact that is used in literature to describe fictional characters as well as in nonfiction, such as when describing a group's *sinister* plans to invade another's territory.

CONSIDERATIONS BEYOND TIER TWO

There is nothing scientific about the way words are identified for attention in school materials. Some words are obvious candidates, such as selecting the word *representation* for a social studies unit on the American Revolutionary War era. But beyond the words that play major roles, choices about what specific set of words to teach are quite arbitrary. Teachers should feel free to use their best judgment, based on an understanding of their students' needs, in selecting words to teach. They should also feel free to treat words in different ways. As Chapters 3, 4, and 5 will show, Tier Two words are not only words that are important for students to know, they are also words that can be worked with in a variety of ways so that students have opportunities to build rich representations of them and of their connections to other words and concepts.

In many texts, however, there may be several unfamiliar words that do not meet the criteria for Tier Two words but which nevertheless require some attention if students are to understand a selection. Consider the following excerpt from the short story "My Father, the Entomologist" (Edwards, 2001, p. 5):

> *"Oh, Bea, you look as lovely as a <u>longhorn beetle</u> lifting off for flight. And I must admit your <u>antennae</u> are adorable. Yes, you've <u>metamorphosed</u> into a <u>splendid</u> young lady."*
>
> *Bea rolled her eyes and <u>muttered</u>, "My father, the <u>entomologist</u>."*
>
> *"I heard that, Bea. It's not nice to <u>mumble</u>. Unless you want to be called a . . . Mumble Bea!" Bea's father slapped his knee and hooted. Bea rolled her eyes a second time.*
>
> *The first day of fifth grade, and my father tells me I look like a longhorn beetle. Bea <u>shuddered</u> at the thought. She absolutely <u>detested</u> bugs.*

Why does Dad have to be <u>obsessed</u> with insects? She wondered. Why not football or golf like most fathers? The answer was simple. Bea's dad was weird. His weirdness made the whole family weird. And he had made Bea the weirdest of all when he named her Bea Ursula Gentry . . . B.U.G.

Suddenly, Bea felt angry. She flew into the kitchen where her father sat reading Insectology. *She <u>hurled</u> her backpack onto the table.*

"You know what, Dad?" she asked, tugging on one of her pigtails. "these are not antennae! Your bumper sticker, 'Have you hugged a bug today?' is not cool! And I <u>despise</u> eating in the dining room with all those dead bugs pinned to the walls!"

With fourth- and fifth-grade students in mind, we have divided the 12 underlined words from the story into the following three categories:

longhorn beetle	*obsessed*	*splendid*
antennae	*detest*	*shuddered*
metamorphosed	*despise*	*mumble*
entomologist	*muttered*	
	hurl	

The first column contains words that are important to the story but that can be dealt with very quickly. *Longhorn beetle* does not call for attention—students will understand it as a type of insect, and more knowledge is not needed to understand the story.

Antennae and *entomologist* are needed to understand the situation the author uses to set up the story, but the two words can be quickly described as "those things that stick out from an insect's head" and "a scientist who studies insects." More precise information is not required for this selection.

Metamorphosed can be explained as simply changed or grown, but to get the humor intended here, the information needs to be given that it is the type of change that certain insects go through, such as when a caterpillar changes into a butterfly. But, again, no more precision is required, and this is not the place to go through the elaborate explanation about the process or how it occurs. That should occur in a science unit about insects.

The words in the next two columns have more general applications

and are consistent with Tier Two words. The words in the second column—*obsessed, detest,* and *despise*—are most substantively related to
the plot of the story, which is about a father who is obsessed with bugs
and his daughter who detests and despises them. *Detest* and *despise* create a kind of "two-fer" situation, in that they are very close synonyms
that could be introduced together and used interchangeably.

The rest of the words do not play key roles in the story, nor is their
unfamiliarity likely to interfere with comprehension. So, which other
words are attended to, if any, is simply a matter of choice and conve-
nience. That is, a decision as to the number of words taught might be
made on the basis of how many a teacher wants to make room for at the
moment. Factors in this decision may include, for example, how large
the current vocabulary load is in the classroom, the time of year, and the
number and difficulty of other concepts presently being dealt with in the
curriculum.

Assume that there is room for several more words from this story. It
might be convenient to teach *splendid* and *shuddered,* because they
could take advantage of concepts already established for the story. *Shuddered* fits well, since something that is detested might well make one
shudder. *Splendid* is also a good fit, as in: "Bea's dad thinks bugs are
splendid, but Bea detests them." Or "If you're obsessed about something, you might think it's splendid." These two words would also be fa-
vored because they have a bit more dimension to them than *mumble,
muttered,* or *hurl.* This is not to say that *mumble, muttered,* or *hurl*
should not be taught, but simply that, presented with the choice of
words to work with, *splendid* and *shuddered* seem to lend themselves to
a wider diversity of possible uses.

WHAT IF THERE ARE NOT ENOUGH WORDS?

Now let us consider a text that does not seem to offer much for vocabulary development because all of the words in the text are familiar to
students. An approach in such a case could be selecting words whose
concepts fit in with the story even though the words do not appear.
For example, if the story features a character who is a loner, introduce
the words *hermit, isolated,* or *solitary;* if a problem is dealt with, present it as a *dilemma* or *conflict;* if a character is hardworking, consider if

he or she is *diligent* and *conscientious*. Think in terms of words that coordinate with, expand, or play off of words, situations, or characters in a text.

Bringing in words whose concepts fit with a story is especially salient when young children are just learning to read and there are only the simplest words in their text. Consider a story in which two children (Pam and Matt) try on a number silly hats, some of which are very big and two of which are exactly alike. A number of words came to mind, and we chose *absurd*, *enormous*, and *identical*. Next we suggest how those words might be introduced to young children:

- In the story, Pam and Matt had very, very silly hats. Another way to say that something is very, very silly is to say that it is *absurd*. When something is *absurd*, it is so silly it's hard to believe.
- Some of the hats that Pam and Matt wore were so big that all you could see were their feet. Another way to say that something is very, very big is to say that it is *enormous*. *Enormous* means "very big—very, very big."
- Pam and Matt put on red hats that were almost exactly alike. A way to say that two things are exactly alike is to say that they are *identical*. *Identical* means "exactly alike."

Words don't need to be completely unfamiliar to students in order to be good candidates for instructional attention. Words might be selected for attention that may be familiar to students but which illustrate the power of an author's choice of words to reveal information about a character or situation. For example, notice the underlined words in the following excerpt, which is taken from a sixth-grade unit on Egypt (Banks et al., 1997, p. 87). The topic is Hatshepsut, a female pharaoh.

Hatshepsut

Hatshepsut was a princess and the wife of a pharaoh. She <u>seized</u> the chance to become pharaoh herself when her husband died. Her young stepson was supposed to become the new pharaoh of Egypt. Hatshepsut proclaimed, however, that the ten-year-old boy was too young to rule on his own. In this way she succeeded in being named co-ruler.

Hatshepsut's Trading Journey

In the eighth year of her reign, Hatshepsut organized the biggest trading expedition of her career. An expedition is a group of people who go on a trip for a set reason. The goal of Hatshepsut's expedition was to trade with Egypt's neighbors to the south in Punt. Historians think Punt may have been in what is today Ethiopia or Somalia. . . .

The huge caravan of scribes, soldiers, artists, and attendants set off along a dusty road that led east to the Red Sea. There they loaded their cargo onto five <u>sleek</u> ships for the long journey south.

The only word identified for attention by the publisher in this segment is *expedition*, which is explained within the text. The two underlined words—*seized* and *sleek*—offer possibilities for drawing students' attention to the effect of an author's choice of words and help the topic come alive.

That Hatshepsut "seized" the chance to become pharaoh reveals something about her character that would make for an interesting discussion. For example: "It says that Hatshepsut seized the chance to become pharaoh. *Seize* means 'to grab something or take control of it firmly.' So, what does that tell us about Hatshepsut? Was she afraid of being pharaoh? Do you think she was eager to become a ruler?"

Similarly, that the expedition sailed off in "sleek" ships communicates the prosperity and style of the Egyptian civilization. Discussion could prompt thinking in that direction: "*Sleek* is a word used to describe something graceful and stylish, that marks its owner as well-to-do. 'They sailed off in sleek ships.' What picture does that give us of Egypt?" Additionally, words like *ambitious* and *calculating* could be introduced to characterize Hatshepsut.

AN EXAMPLE FOR OLDER STUDENTS

The examples provided thus far were drawn from texts for readers in the intermediate grades. Although the same principles apply to selecting words from texts for students in the upper grades, they may play out a bit differently. Thus, we present a discussion of the words that might be selected for Agatha Christie's "In a Glass Darkly" (1934), a story that is likely to be of interest to students in eighth or ninth grade. It is a rather brooding tale that moves from a murderous premonition to unrequited love, jealousy, and near tragedy before resolving happily. The story begins as the narrator, while staying with a friend, sees a vision of a man strangling a woman. The woman turns out to be his friend's sister, Sylvia, with whom he falls in love. But Sylvia is engaged—to the man he saw in his vision. He tells her of the vision, and she breaks her engagement. For years, the narrator is unable to tell her of his feelings for her. Finally, love is revealed and they marry. But he is deeply jealous, a feeling that results in his nearly strangling his wife—until he notices in the mirror that he is playing out the scene of his premonition.

The language of the story is sophisticated but not particularly difficult. Most words will likely be at least passingly familiar to many readers in eighth or ninth grade. However, many of the words are probably not of high frequency in the students' vocabularies, and thus an opportunity presents itself for students to work with these words and gain fluency with them. Here are the 30 words from the story that we identified as Tier Two words:

essential	*appreciated*	*altered*
intervened	*decent*	*well-off*
attractive	*rambling*	*prospect*
valet	*throttling*	*complication*
gravely	*upshot*	*leisure*
disinterested	*scornfully*	*devotedly*
absurdly	*endangering*	*inevitable*
entrenched	*gloomy*	*sullen*
savage	*unwarranted*	*abuse*
endurance	*revelation*	*sobering*

Of the 30 words, we decided to focus on 10 of them: *essential, altered, well-off, devoted, entrenched, inevitable, sobering, revelation, upshot,* and *disinterested.*

Ten words may be a lot to develop effectively for one story, but we see it as a workable number because many of them will already be familiar. Also, two of the words could be introduced rather briefly with little or no follow-up work. These are *altered,* which could be defined simply as "permanently changed," and *well-off,* which could simply be given the synonym *wealthy*. The reason for attention to these two words is that they could cause confusion at the local level in the story if not understood.

Two other words were also chosen because they could cause confusion in a part of the story. These are *upshot* and *disinterested*. The narrator talks of the *upshot* of his decision to tell Sylvia that he saw a vision of her fiancé choking her. Because of the context and feel of the story, we thought *upshot* might be interpreted as some sort of physical violence, instead of simply "the result of." The word *disinterested* meaning "not being involved in a particular situation" is often confused with *uninterested*, meaning "not interested," and the story provides a good opportunity to introduce that distinction.

Five words seem to convey the mood and emotional impact of story developments: *devoted, entrenched, inevitable, sobering*, and *revelation*. And the word *essential* was chosen because "one essential detail" turns out to be a key plot device—that is, in his premonition, the narrator notices a scar on the left side of the choker's face. The essential detail he fails to account for is that he is seeing this in a mirror, so the scar is actually on the right. The five words can be used to describe the plot as follows: The narrator is *devoted* to Sylvia, although *entrenched* in a jealousy that causes *inevitable* problems. Only a *sobering revelation* (that *essential* detail) saves him, his marriage, and his wife.

A couple of points should be emphasized here. The words were selected not so much because they are essential to comprehension of the story but because they seem most closely integral to the mood and plot. In this way, the vocabulary work provides both for learning new words and for enriching understanding of literature. This decision was made possible because there was a large pool of words from which to choose. Sometimes choices are more limited, and sometimes the best words are not so tied to the story. In such cases, a decision might be made to select words that seem most productive for vocabulary development despite their role in the story.

For the six words we consider to be most important to teach, some characteristics of the words themselves also drove our selections. *Sobering* was selected because its strongest sense for students might be as the opposite of drunk. So, the context of the story provides a good opportunity to overcome that and introduce its more general sense. The others, *essential, devoted, entrenched, inevitable*, and *revelation*, have wide potential for use and are not limited to specific situations or stereotypical contexts. Yet, they seem to be strongly expressive words that can bring emotional impact to contexts in which they are used.

AN EXAMPLE FOR YOUNG CHILDREN

We turn now to selecting words to enhance the vocabulary repertoires of young children—those who are just learning to read. We make two immediate distinctions between vocabulary work with intermediate and older students and work with students in the earliest grades, typically kindergarten though early second grade. The first is that we consider the best sources for new vocabulary to be trade books that teachers read aloud to children rather than the books children read on their own. In Chapter 4 we will make our case for that position. The second distinction is that in contrast to introducing words before a story, in our work with young children we have found it most appropriate to engage in vocabulary activities after a story has been read.

There are two reasons we decided that vocabulary activities for young children should occur after a story. First, if a word is needed for comprehension, since the teacher is reading the story she is available to briefly explain the word at the point in the story where it is needed (e.g., "A *ukulele* is a kind of guitar"; or "When ducks *molt*, they lose their feathers and can't fly until new ones grow"). Second, since the words that will be singled out for vocabulary attention are words that are very likely unfamiliar to young children, the context from the story provides a rich example of the word's use and thus strong support for the children's initial learning of the word.

The basis for selecting words from trade books for young children is that they are Tier Two words and words that are not too difficult to explain to young children. Here, we present our thinking for selecting three words for instructional attention from *The Popcorn Dragon* (Thayer, 1953), a story targeted to kindergartners.

In our review of *The Popcorn Dragon* for Tier Two candidate words, we first identified the following seven: *accidentally, drowsy, pranced, scorched, envious, delighted,* and *forlorn.* From the pool of seven, we decided to provide instruction for three: *envious, delighted,* and *forlorn.* We considered three issues in making our choices. First, we determined that the concept represented by each word was understandable to kindergartners; that is, 5-year-olds understand the concepts of wanting something someone else has *(envious)*, being very happy *(delighted)*, and being very sad *(forlorn)*. Second, it is not too difficult to explain the meanings of those words in very simple language, as illustrated in the previous sentence! And, third, each word has extensive possibilities for use. In particular, the words are found in numerous fairy tales; that is, there is often some character who is envious of another, and there are characters who are delighted or forlorn about the turn of events. The words, however, are not restricted to make-believe; they can all be used in describing people in common situations.

We found the other candidate words—*pranced, accidentally, scorched,* and *drowsy*—interesting and potentially useful, but we saw *scorched* and *pranced* as narrower than the ones we chose, and *drowsy* and *accidentally* as not quite so interesting. We hasten to make the point that this is all a matter of judgment. The final decisions about which words to teach may not be as important as thoughtful consideration about why to teach certain words and not others.

WHAT ABOUT WORDS BEING ON GRADE LEVEL?

A concern that surfaces in deciding which words to teach is whether words are appropriate for students at certain grade levels. Key to this concern is to understand that no formula exists for selecting age-appropriate vocabulary words despite lists that identify "fifth-grade words" or "seventh-grade words." There is simply no basis for determining which words students should be learning at different grade levels. For example, that *coincidence* is an "eighth-grade word" according to a frequency index means only that most students do not know the word until eighth grade. It does not mean that students in seventh or even third grade cannot learn the word or should not be taught it.

There are only two things that make a word inappropriate for a certain level. One is not being able to explain the meaning of a word in known terms. If the words used to explain a target word are likely unknown to the students, then the word is too hard. The other consideration for word selection is that the words be useful and interesting—ones that students will be able to find uses for in their everyday lives. Of course, this is a matter of judgment, best decided by those who know the individual students. Work we have done with kindergarten and first-grade children shows that sophisticated words can be successfully taught to young children. For example, kindergartners readily applied *nuisance* to disruptive classmates, and understood what was happening when a *commotion* occurred in the hall; first graders could easily discern *argumentative* peers from those who acted *dignified*!

IN SUMMARY

In evaluating words as possible candidates for instruction, here are three things to keep in mind:

1. How generally useful is the word? Is it a word that students are likely to meet often in other texts? Will it be of use to students in describing their own experiences?

For example, students are likely to find more situations in which to apply *typical* and *dread* than *portage* and *brackish*.

2. How does the word relate to other words, to ideas that students know or have been learning? Does it directly relate to some topic of study in the classroom? Or might it add a dimension to ideas that have been developed?

For example, what might knowing the word *hubris* bring to a middle school student's understanding of the battles at Lexington and Concord, which set the Revolutionary War in motion?

3. What does the word bring to a text or situation? What role does the word play in communicating the meaning of the context in which it is used?

A word's meaning might be necessary for understanding a text. Or understanding its meaning might allow an enriched insight about the situation being presented, such as in the case of Hatshepsut's seizing power and her expedition traveling in sleek ships.

Keep in mind that there is no formula for selecting age-appropriate vocabulary words despite lists that identify "fifth-grade words" or "seventh-grade words." As long as the word can be explained in known words and can apply to what students might talk or write about, it is an appropriate word to teach.

▪ *Your Turn* ▪

We invite you to use what you have learned in this chapter to make some decisions about which words you will teach.

1. Select a text that your students will be reading. It can be a story, or an excerpt from a chapter book or novel, or a social studies textbook.
2. List all the words that are likely to be unfamiliar to students.
3. Analyze the word list:
   - Which words can be categorized as Tier Two words?
   - Which of the Tier Two words are most necessary for comprehension?
   - Are there other words needed for comprehension? Which ones?
4. On the basis of your analysis, which words will you teach?
   - Which will need only brief attention?
   - Which will you give more elaborate attention to?

CHAPTER 3

Introducing Vocabulary

Ms. T's classroom, Monday morning:

Ms. T: Our first vocabulary word is *covet*. Sam, what does *covet* mean?

SAM: (*reading from the dictionary/glossary*) "To wish for greatly or with envy."

Ms. T: Okay. So, if someone has a CD, and you really wish you had it, we might say that you covet the CD. Let's look at the next word. . . .

Ms. T's classroom, Thursday morning:

MARIA: (*reading from a story*) "As much as Philip liked his new bike, he coveted his cousin's shiny scooter."

Ms. T: *Covet* is one of our vocabulary words. Who remembers what it means? Terry?

TERRY: No response.

Ms. T: Alex?

ALEX: Umm . . .

Ms. T: Alison?

ALISON: Uh, I think, like making a wish. He made a wish to get a scooter, but his parents got him a bike instead.

The above exchange typifies events that sometimes occur in relation to vocabulary instruction. Although a word's definition is explicitly provided, students often do not recall it several days later, or what is recalled is a somewhat misleading interpretation of the word's meaning. The purpose of this chapter is to discuss reasons that this might occur and to present ways to make vocabulary introduction more effective.

INTRODUCING WORDS IS THE FIRST STEP

The title of this chapter is *introducing* vocabulary to make the point that providing word-meaning information is only a first step in building word knowledge. Just providing information—even rich, meaningful explanations—will not result in deep or sustained knowledge of a word. Multiple encounters over time are called for if the goal is more than a temporary surface-level understanding and if new words are to become permanently and flexibly represented in students' vocabulary repertoires. In the two chapters that follow this one, the focus will be on what teachers can do after initial word introduction to promote rich and sustained knowledge. Here, our focus is how to initially present words in ways that help them take root in students' vocabularies.

Before we open the discussion of how to effectively initiate building students' understanding of word meanings, we consider for a moment the situations in which words are likely to be introduced in the classroom. The most common is before a text is read. The reasoning behind this is to make unfamiliar words available for students when they encounter them as they read. If students are most often reading text independently, introducing word meanings that are important to comprehension before reading is the reasonable choice. Certainly this makes sense in contrast to waiting until after reading to introduce the words.

PROVIDING INITIAL WORD MEANING INFORMATION THROUGH DEFINITIONS

If one asks teachers how they first introduce a word, there is a high probability that *definition* will be in their responses. Indeed, definitions are synonymous with vocabulary instruction in many classrooms. However, the reality is that definitions are not an effective vehicle for learning word meanings. Studies that provided dictionary definitions to students and asked students to create sentences with the words or answers to brief questions about the words revealed that—

- Sixty-three percent of the students' sentences were judged to be "odd" (Miller & Gildea, 1985).
- Sixty percent of students' responses were unacceptable (McKeown, 1991, 1993).
- Students frequently interpreted one or two words from a definition as the entire meaning (Scott & Nagy, 1989).

Problems with Dictionary Definitions

To understand why dictionary definitions are so often unhelpful, it can be useful to know a bit about how definitions end up in the form they do. Formalized definitional practice can be traced to the time of Samuel Johnson's mid-18th-century *Dictionary of the English Language*. The traditional form of definitions is based on describing a word by first identifying the class to which something belongs and then indicating how it differs from other members of the class. A classic example is *bachelor* defined as *"a man* who is *unmarried."*

The most overriding consideration for definitional format, however, is that definitions in dictionaries must be concise because of space restrictions. Lexicographers, those who develop dictionaries, have called this constraint "horrendous." Indeed, one lexicographer made the point that "almost every defining characteristic common to dictionaries can be traced to the need to conserve space " (Landau, 1984, p. 140), and another has said that dictionary definitions have led to "some remarkable convolutions in dictionary prose style" (Hanks, 1987, p. 120).

So there is nothing "official" or "scientific" about the form in which definitions appear. For this reason, combined with the fact that definitions are not particularly helpful for student learning, we prefer to introduce new vocabulary by explaining a word's meaning rather than providing a definition for the word.

When we examined definitions by putting ourselves in the place of a young learner trying to make sense of the information, we came up with four characteristic features of definitions that get in the way of understanding word meaning.

The first we called **weak differentiation**, which means that the definition does not differentiate how the target word is different from other similar words—how it is a specific case of a more general idea. For example, consider *conspicuous* defined in a junior dictionary as "easily seen." This definition weakly differentiates *conspicuous* from the general domain of "visible." After all, unless it is dark or one has poor vision, nearly everything is easily seen. Something conspicuous is not just easy to see but rather pops out at you because of its size or color or inappropriateness to a situation.

Second problem of dictionary definitions is that they are often stated in such **vague language** that they provide little information. As an example, consider *typical* defined as "being a type." At best, a learner might manage to ask, "A type of what?" It is unlikely that a young student would make enough sense of the definition to develop much, if any, idea of what *typical* means.

A third problem of definitions is that there may be a **more likely interpretation** of meaning than the one intended. This can happen when a definition uses familiar words in unfamiliar ways. For example, consider the definition for *devious*: "straying from the right course; not straightforward." The idea of straying from a course is likely to be interpreted in a concrete, physical way. A young learner may conclude that *devious* has to do with crooked walking or getting lost.

The fourth problematic characteristic is that some definitions give **multiple pieces of information** but offer no guidance in how they should be integrated. For example, consider the definition for *exotic*: "foreign; strange; not native." A learner might wonder what relationship to draw among these parts. Is something exotic if it is strange but not foreign?—Or only if it is both foreign and strange? The concept for *exotic* that needs to be captured is that when something is exotic it may be strange or unusual or special *because* it comes from a distant place.

The problematic features of dictionary definitions as exemplified by those provided above, the evidence that young students do not learn effectively from dictionary definitions, and the complaints of lexicographers themselves all point to a need for those of us who are engaged in teaching to do better than dictionaries may do when presenting word-meaning information. Toward this goal, we present three constructs for developing *initial* word-meaning information: student-friendly explanations of words, instructional contexts, and opportunities for students to interact with word meanings in ways that oblige them to think about what a word means.

▪ *You Try It* ▪

Select a few words that are unfamiliar to your students, and ask them to look up the words in a classroom dictionary and read the definitions. Then, ask students to talk about what they think the definition means. What was most helpful to them in understanding the definition? What was confusing?

Developing Student-Friendly Explanations

Giving a definition of a word—even for words we know well—is not an easy task. Toward developing student-friendly explanations, two basic principles should be followed: (1) Characterize the word and how it is typically used. (2) Explain the meaning in everyday language.

Characterize the Word

For an explanation to be optimally helpful, it should be as particular as possible. It should pinpoint a word's meaning by explaining its typical use. Ask yourself, "When do I use *this word* particularly?" Also, "Why do we have such a word?" In some cases, an explanation that pinpoints a word's meaning may not capture all possible applications of that word. But explanations that attempt to be all-inclusive sacrifice explanatory strength. It is preferable to start students off with a strong focused concept of what a word means rather than draw attention to multiple senses of meaning. Rather than dealing with too much information at the outset, language users can more readily extend a concept as their use of it grows.

As an exercise in characterization, consider the word *tamper.* What comes to mind when you think of that word? Possibly that if you tamper with something it doesn't work any more; also, that tampering is often done secretly to try to trick or harm someone. But consider a definition for *tamper* taken from a dictionary: "to interfere in a secret or incorrect way." This definition would seem to include simply meddling in some-one else's affairs as a busybody. It lacks the sense of messing up some-thing in a possibly sinister way. A more student-friendly explanation, crafted to highlight the notion that tampering with something damages it, might be "to change something secretly so that it does not work prop-erly or becomes harmful."

Explain Meanings in Everyday Language

Developing effective word explanations for students calls for taking care to explain the concept in language that is readily accessible so students can understand the concept with ease. Definitions such as "one associ-ated with another" are more puzzling than helpful. What word comes to mind when you read that definition? (The word is *ally*!)

To move the definition of *ally* into accessible language, think of how to communicate the concept of "association" in student-friendly terms. Perhaps something like "somebody who does things with you" or "some-body you hang around with." Now, consider whether that captures the characteristic meaning of *ally*: It seems to miss the role of an ally as help-ing in some common cause. Picking up on that aspect, we might come up with a definition such as "someone who helps you in what you are trying to do, especially when there are other people who are against you."

Another aspect of creating an explanation with an eye toward ac-cessible language is developing it in such a way that students will at-tend to the whole explanation. This is to ensure that some words within an explanation do not take on unintended emphasis and lead students to choose just part of the explanation as the entire meaning. For instance, explaining *meticulous* as "extremely or excessively careful about small details" gives prominence to the word *careful*. Using the most obvious sense of *careful*, students could interpret the word as re-lating to being cautious about danger. Adding *neat* might help students understand the appropriate sense of *careful*. A student-friendly form of the definition might then be given as "being very neat and careful about small details."

Consider a few more words and how we might work our way from dictionary definitions to student-friendly explanations.

covert: kept from sight; secret; hidden
What are students likely to make of this definition? The clearest part, for students, would seem to be the word *secret*. So, students might well interpret the word as a synonym for *secret* without even stopping to realize that the word is an adjective rather than a noun. Beyond this possible misinterpretation, the definition sounds as if it applies to something or someone that you want to hide. This is at odds with the way *covert* is most often used—to describe an action done in a secretive way. To define *covert* as "**describes something that is done in a hidden or secret way**" makes it much clearer to students how the word is to be applied.

disrupt: break up; split
This could easily be interpreted as physical breaking, as in "We disrupted the candy bar so we could all share it." What's the nature of *disrupt* that needs to be captured? It would seem to be that disrupting is like rudely stopping something that's going on, or causing a problem that makes some activity cease. Using these ideas might lead to the student-friendly explanation: "**to cause difficulties that stop something from continuing easily or peacefully.**"

illusion: appearance or feeling that misleads because it is not real
This is a good example of a vague definition. An "appearance that misleads" is rather hard to make sense of. Might it be something that looks good but isn't—like a stale piece of cake? Or considering "feeling"—how does a feeling mislead? How is a feeling not real? The core of *illusion* is something that looks real but isn't, or appears to be something but isn't there at all. Those ideas could be put together in a definition such as "**something that looks like one thing but is really something else or is not there at all.**"

improvise: to make, invent, or arrange with whatever is on hand
This definition seems to lack a key component of improvisation, the idea that you use whatever is on hand *because* you don't have exactly what's called for. Also, the "make, invent, or arrange" trio makes the whole concept a bit vague. A definition that better characterizes *improvise* and is more concrete and accessible might be

"**to make something you need by using whatever is available at the moment.**"

morbid: not healthy or normal
This definition really pushes the limits of failing to characterize a word! Something morbid is well beyond not healthy. Imagine a student telling his mother, "I think I need to stay home from school today—I'm feeling morbid"! The definition has to be explicit about the connection to death or gruesome thoughts. Perhaps a more student-friendly explanation is "**showing a great interest in horrible, gruesome details, especially about death.**"

Note that all the above student-friendly explanations are quite a bit longer than their dictionary counterparts. The brevity of many dictionary definitions leaves too much assumed, and young learners often make incorrect assumptions or are unable to put the ideas together at all. Fuller, more explicit language is needed to promote students' development of word meaning. As teachers, we do not have the constraints imposed on lexicographers, so we can provide the kinds of explanations that will be most helpful to students.

If you review the student-friendly explanations above, you will also notice that they often include words such as *something, someone,* or *describes*. These terms anchor the meaning for students so they can begin to get an idea of how to use the word.

▪ *You Try It* ▪

You might find it useful to try your hand at creating some student-friendly explanations.

1. Select some words that your students are currently learning.
2. Look up the definitions for the words provided in a dictionary or glossary.
3. Think about the definitions from a young learner's point of view.
   - What difficulties might the definitions pose to such a learner? (Refer to pages 33 and 34 for a discussion of potential definition difficulties.)

- How might you characterize the words so that their meanings are specific?
- What everyday language might you use to craft explanations?

4. Create student-friendly explanations for the words you selected. Try to include the words *something, someone,* or *describes* in your explanations.
5. Share the explanations you created with your students. Ask them to compare your explanations with the definitions provided in a dictionary or glossary.

PROVIDING MEANING INFORMATION THROUGH INSTRUCTIONAL CONTEXTS

Another common way to convey word-meaning information is through instructional contexts. In contrast to natural contexts, which were discussed in Chapter 1, instructional contexts refer to contexts that have been developed with the intention of providing strong clues to a word's meaning. To understand how different the two types of context are, consider the natural context in which the word *grudgingly* appeared in Chapter 1, contrasted with an instructional context.

"Every step she takes is so perfect and graceful," Ginny said *grudgingly,* as she watched Sandra dance.

The use of grudgingly makes sense—it communicates well—*if* you know the meaning of the word. However, the natural context is misleading for readers who do not know the meaning because the situation described might lead such readers to think that grudgingly refers to a positive feeling such as admiration. In contrast to the misleading natural context in which *grudgingly* was found, one could develop an instructional context in which the meaning elements of *grudgingly* are made clear and from which its meaning is more easily derived. For example:

Ginny hated the way Sandra always danced so beautifully. "No matter how much I practice, I never do it as well. Every step Sandra takes is so perfect and graceful," Ginny said *grudgingly*.

Helping students derive word meaning from natural contexts will be discussed fully in Chapter 6. Here, we focus on instructional contexts, which are developed by teachers and available in teacher guides for textbooks.

Even though instructional contexts are designed to make word meaning transparent, it is not enough to simply make an instructional context available to students. In one way or another, a definition or explanation of the target word needs to be developed. And the reasoning behind deriving a meaning for the target word needs to be made public for students. Mere exposure to an instructional context leaves introduction of word meaning incomplete. There is no guarantee that students will come to a clear or correct conclusion about a word's meaning. Making word-meaning information public ensures that all students will begin with a clear, explicit concept of the word. And making public how word meaning was derived from the context allows students to build a stronger connection between the word and its meaning.

For example, if a student derives the meaning of *grudgingly* and provides an adequate definition, perhaps "saying something that you really don't like saying," the teacher needs to probe that student's thinking in ways that require the students to explain the parts that helped him or her figure out that Ginny really didn't want to say what she said. So, let's go back into Ms. T's class and see what such an exchange might be like:

Ms. T: Tell us how you figured out that Ginny said it grudgingly because it was something she didn't like saying.

Tonia: Well, she didn't like that Sandra always danced so good.

Ms. T: She didn't? Why not?

Tonia: Because *she* didn't.

Lee: And Ginny practiced a lot, and still didn't.

Zoe: So she was jealous, probably.

Ms. T: *Jealous* is a good word to use here. So, Ginny said Sandra danced well, but she said it grudgingly. She really didn't want to admit that Sandra was such a good dancer.

Explaining their reasoning may be quite difficult for students. Therefore, it is a good idea to start out by having the teacher provide some models for deriving meaning from instructional contexts. As an example, consider the following:

> The rider couldn't control the *obstinate* horse. She was getting angry that this horse acted this way often.

Modeling how one might derive the meaning for *obstinate* could go something like this:

> *Obstinate* must mean something that a horse could be, and it has to be something that would make a horse hard to control. Maybe scared, a horse could be scared, and because he was scared, he might act up and be hard to control. But it says the horse acted this way often and that the rider was angry about it. I don't think a rider would be angry at a scared horse. *Obstinate* must be a way a horse acts that riders don't like. It could mean stubborn, because horses can get stubborn and some horses can get stubborn often. When they do, it's hard for a rider to get them to do what she wants.

Such modeling can be useful, but teachers should use it sparingly because it puts students in the passive role of overhearing the teacher thinking aloud. However, such modeling is appropriate when students are being introduced to the idea of deriving meaning from context and when a complicated and subtle context is being explored. It is important, however, to emphasize that students should be made part of the deriving-meaning process as soon as possible, queried along the way as meaning elements are derived from a context.

The following examples show how one might scaffold students' attempts to derive word meanings from instructional contexts:

> The deer would be able to eat all they wanted in the meadow, for there was an *abundance* of grass.
>
> - Why would the deer be able to eat all they wanted?
> - How much grass must be in the meadow?
> - So, what do you think *abundance* means?

> The train ride had been long, and I was tired of looking out the window. So I decided to *eavesdrop* on what two of the passengers sit-

ting behind me were saying. I knew what they were saying was none of my business, but it might be interesting, so I tried to listen.

- What is this person up to? What told you that?
- What's this about it was none of his business?
- So, *eavesdrop* means what kind of listening?

"Please don't eat the flowers, sir," said the waiter. "I don't think they are *edible*! They might make you sick!"

- What is the waiter telling the man about the flowers?
- If eating them might make you sick, what does that tell you?
- So, if you shouldn't eat things that are not edible, what does *edible* mean?

▪ *You Try It* ▪

You might find it useful to try your hand at creating some instructional contexts for words that you want your students to learn. Develop some sentences about each target word, as well as some questions to help students make use of the information to derive its meaning.

PROVIDING MEANINGS AS WORDS
ARE ENCOUNTERED

The assumption to this point has been that words are introduced before a text is read, and certainly if students are most often reading text independently, introducing word meanings that are important to comprehension before reading is the reasonable choice. This makes sense in contrast to waiting until after reading to introduce the words. But if the word is likely to affect comprehension of the story, then the most effective place to introduce word meaning may be at the moment the word is met in the text. The meaning can then be integrated into the context of use immediately, which provides strong support for comprehension. In this way, students are not called upon to put comprehension on hold as they access their memories for the word's meaning. Another important consideration is that, even if students have been introduced to a word's meaning before reading, their memory for a newly introduced word meaning may still be rather tentative, making it difficult to bring that meaning into the text.

At times when a text is read aloud in class, introducing the meanings of words as they are encountered during reading can be done simply and briefly by giving a quick explanation of the word or what it means within the context. For example, consider the following context from *Roll of Thunder, Hear My Cry* (Taylor, 1976, p. 4): "Christopher-John and Stacey were not too pleased about the clothing or school either. Only Little Man, just beginning his school career, found the prospects of both intriguing." At this point, a teacher could simply say, "*Intriguing* means Little Man was pretty interested in and excited about school."

Another approach to dealing with word meanings as text is read might be to ask students for the meaning of a potentially unfamiliar word that is encountered, bringing them into the deriving-meaning process as described in the previous section. However, it is important to provide guidance if students do not quickly know the word's meaning. Otherwise, it can lead to students making guesses, many of which may be incorrect. That can both take attention to the text offtrack as well as confuse students as to the actual meaning of the word.

Here, the point is teacher guidance. Certainly, allow students to figure out clues to a word's meaning from contexts, but don't let them stray too far before stepping in, either to give the meaning or to point out the relevant clues or how to interpret them. For example, consider the following exchange around a context from Roald Dahl's *Charlie and the Great Glass Elevator* (1972, p. 88):

Through the glass floor of the Elevator, Charlie caught a quick glimpse of the huge red roof and the tall chimneys of the giant factory. They were plunging straight down onto it.

Ms. T:	What do you think *glimpse* means?
Jen:	Like a piece of something.
Ms. T:	A piece of something?
Jen:	Yeah. I think a piece of the roof or the chimney came in and hit him.
Ms. T:	Oh, I see how you could get that idea. But *glimpse* means "a quick look at something, kind of a peek." So, he was just getting a quick look at the roof and chimney as the Elevator fell.

Note how Ms. T turns back Jen's original surmise about the word's meaning, giving Jen an opportunity to explain where that came from. That gives Ms. T an understanding of how Jen reached that conclusion. So, Ms. T is able to acknowledge Jen's thinking while explaining how the actual meaning of glimpse fits the context.

ENGAGING STUDENTS IN DEALING WITH WORD MEANINGS

Providing student-friendly explanations or scaffolding students as they derive word meanings from instructional contexts is only part of what it takes to help students establish an initial understanding of what a word means. The other part is to ensure that students actually deal with the meanings right away. There are numerous short and lively activities that can require students to process meanings. We next provide several that we have found to be engaging for students. The activities below come from the vocabulary research studies that we engaged in and which we noted in Chapter 1.

Word Associations

After having presented explanations for *accomplice, virtuoso, philanthropist*, and *novice*, we asked students to associate one of their new words with a presented word or phrase, such as the following:

- Which word goes with crook? (*accomplice*)
- Which word goes with "gift to build a new hospital"? (*philanthropist*)
- Which word goes with piano? (*virtuoso*)
- Which word goes with kindergartner? (*novice*)

In each case, students were then asked *why* they decided on the connection they had made. Associating a known word with a newly learned word reinforces even further the meaning of the word. Note that the associations are not synonyms; rather, the student must develop a relationship. For example, in the case of associations between *crook* and *accomplice*, one student might say that an accomplice helps a crook, another might say that an accomplice is learning to be a crook, and yet another might suggest that crooks want accomplices to help them in their wrongdoings. Having students explain their reasoning is an essential component of the kind of instruction that requires learners to process information—directly deal with information by considering and mentally manipulating it.

Have You Ever . . . ?

This activity helps students associate newly learned words with contexts and activities from their own experience. Thus, it helps students understand that they have a place for the word in their vocabularies. In the activity, students are asked to "Describe a time when you might *urge* someone, *commend* someone, *banter* with someone."

Applause, Applause!

For this activity, students are asked to clap in order to indicate how much they would like (not at all, a little bit, a lot) to be described by the target words: *frank, impish, vain, stern*. And, as always, *why* they would feel that way.

Idea Completions

In contrast to the traditional "write a sentence using the new word," which can result in meaningless use (e.g., "I saw a virtuoso."), we provided students with sentence stems that required them to integrate a word's meaning into a context in order to explain a situation. For example:

> The audience asked the virtuoso to play another piece of music because . . .

> The skiing teacher said Maria was a novice on the ski slopes because . . .

There are many variations on activities that get students actively engaged with word meanings. They can be as simple as asking questions such as the following about newly introduced words:

When might you . . . ?
How might you . . . ?
Why might you . . . ?

The key to effective activities is that they require students to attend to a word's meaning in order to apply it meaningfully to an example situation.

IN SUMMARY

In introducing words, here are some things to keep in mind:

- Make word meanings explicit and clear. Develop student-friendly explanations or create instructional contexts for discussing word meanings.
- Get students actively involved with thinking about and using the meanings right away.

Full understanding and spontaneous, appropriate use of new words develops gradually, but a strong start is essential to allowing those processes to occur.

▪ *Your Turn* ▪

We invite you to use what you have learned in this chapter to develop some ways to introduce words you will teach.

1. Select words from a text that your students will be reading.
2. Create a student-friendly explanation for each word by—
   - Thinking about what specific elements make the word different from other words.
   - Using everyday language.
3. Develop instructional contexts for some words. That is, write sentences and develop questions that will support students in deriving the meaning of those words.
4. Create some activities that will engage students in dealing with the word's meaning.

CHAPTER 4

Developing Vocabulary in the Earliest Grades

The following exchange occurred in a first-grade classroom in February:

JASON: Is this going to be an ordinary day?

Ms. H: What would make it ordinary?

JASON: If we like did the same old thing.

Ms. H: What might make it not ordinary, make it exceptional?

JASON: If you gave us prizes for being good—I mean exceptional and mature.

All of the children in the class of more than 20 students had been having difficulty learning to read, and many of them came from poverty backgrounds. In January, these children were brought together for most of the morning for intensive literacy instruction with a gifted teacher. The teacher had two major goals for the children: (1) They would learn to read. (2) Their listening and speaking vocabularies would be enlarged and enriched. By February, it was not unusual to hear the kind of conversation captured in the above example. The purpose of this chapter is to consider the special case of vocabulary development for young children. It focuses on teaching words from texts that are read aloud to children rather than read by children, and it presents activities that take into account the kind of support that young children need to make sense of those words.

SOURCES OF WORDS FOR YOUNG CHILDREN'S VOCABULARY DEVELOPMENT

We start this chapter by noting where words for young children's vocabulary development do *not* come from—and that is from the text materials that children are asked to read early in the course of reading acquisition. This is because, given beginning readers' word identification limitations, the text materials used in the early phases of learning to read should comprise words children know from oral language, that is, Tier One words like *run* and *ball*. Indeed, learning to read is learning a new representation for the language young children know from speech. As such, the early text materials are not good sources for adding new words to children's vocabulary repertoires. Emphatically, however, this does not mean that adding to and enriching children's vocabulary repertoires should be put on hold; it only means that enriching young children's vocabulary can not be best developed through the words in the materials that young children read themselves.

Young children's listening and speaking competence is in advance of their reading and writing competence. That is, they can understand much more sophisticated content presented in oral language than they can read independently. As children are developing their reading and writing competence, we need to take advantage of their listening and speaking competencies to enhance their vocabulary development. We certainly must not hold back adding vocabulary to children's repertoires until their word recognition becomes adequate. Thus, a major *source* for identifying interesting words are the delightful trade books that are read to children. However, the ideas in the little stories young children read on their own can still be a useful resource. As indicated at the beginning of this chapter, the *words* in the stories are not appropriate for enriching children's vocabularies but some of the *ideas* in the simplest stories can be characterized by sophisticated words. Thus, after a story has been read, the teacher can describe a character or incident with an interesting word. Consider for example, a story in the first book in first grade in which some children make cookies. The story is mostly built around pictures, with the vocabulary limited to some children's names and words such as *pass, pat, pan*, and *cookies*. The story ends with the children eating the cookies and saying, "Mmmm. Good!"

The teacher could remind the children that after the characters in the story ate the cookies they said, "Mmmm. Good!" and explain that another way to say that is that the characters thought the cookies were *scrumptious*. She could explain the word further by saying that when something is scrumptious it tastes great. *Scrumptious* lends itself to a variety of other interactions that children could have with the word. They could be asked to think of foods that they think are scrumptious as well as suggesting foods that they do not think are scrumptious. The notion could go further with asking the children what would be scrumptious to a mouse?—to a cat?

The teacher could also mention that in the story the children ate up all the cookies really quickly, explaining that another way to say that is that they *devoured* the cookies. The children could be asked to suggest foods that they would devour. Even further the teacher might suggest that the reason the children devoured the food is that they were *famished*. So, even though the stories that young readers read do not offer words to teach, the stories are still a resource for the teacher to use in generating target words.

As mentioned earlier, tradebooks that are read aloud to children are excellent sources of sophisticated words, and in recent work we have been able to use them to advantage. Specifically, several years ago, we initiated Text Talk, a research and development project aimed at capturing the benefits of read alouds (Beck & McKeown, 2001; McKeown & Beck, in press). Text Talk has two main goals. One goal is to enhance comprehension through interspersed open questions that asked children to consider the ideas in the story, talk about them, and make connections among them as the story moves along. The second goal is to enhance vocabulary development.

From 80 children's trade books (distributed across kindergarten and first and second grades) that we selected for use in Text Talk, we identified about 1,500 words as potential candidates to teach to children. A word was considered a good candidate if it seemed likely to be unfamiliar to young children and yet a word whose concept they could identify with and use in normal conversation. From that list we pared down our choices and selected about three words per story for direct teaching following a reading of the story. Appendix A lists the books that are used in Text Talk with the words from each book that we singled out for instruction.

Several issues about the books and words need to be emphasized. First, although we think all the books are good children's books, there is nothing exclusive about the books we used. That is, there are many other books that could be chosen. Second, although we selected an average of three words per book, we could have selected more. We considered issues of instructional time and the rate at which books were being read to children, which was one or two a week. As such, we thought that about three words per book was a reasonable number. However, there are many other approaches to determining the number of words taught. For example, if fewer books are read to children, more words from each book might well be identified for instruction.

▪ *You Try It* ▪

Take some time to look over Appendix A. You may have some of the books listed in your personal, classroom, school, or local library. If so, read through one or two of the books to find other words that you might want to consider for teaching. If you are a first- or second-grade teacher, read some of the earliest stories and think about ways of labeling events, characters' qualities, and the like with sophisticated words. Use the criterion we described earlier: The word is unfamiliar to young children, but the concept represented by the word is one they can understand and could use in conversation.

SEQUENCED ACTIVITIES FOR TEACHING WORDS TO YOUNG CHILDREN

In our Text Talk project, direct instruction in vocabulary occurs after a story has been read, discussed, and wrapped up. This provides a strong context with which to begin the word-meaning introduction. But note that in cases where we thought that a word was needed for story comprehension, we suggested that the teacher stop and briefly explain the word during reading. So, for example, in reading *Six-Dinner Sid* (Moore,

1991), when Sid the cat was taken to the vet, the teacher said, "A vet is a special doctor for animals."

Let's consider the vocabulary instruction for *A Pocket for Corduroy* (Freeman, 1978), a story about a teddy bear (Corduroy) who spends the night at a laundromat. All three words meet the criteria for Tier Two words described in Chapter 2 (p. 19). Of particular significance for younger children is the instructional potential of the words—that is, the opportunities the words offer for activities that can help children build a representation of the meaning of the word and of its connections to other words.

As an example of the kinds of instructional suggestions provided to teachers, consider the following activities for *reluctant*:

> In the story, Lisa was *reluctant* to leave the laundromat without Corduroy. *Reluctant* means you are not sure you want to do something. Say the word with me.
>
> Someone might be reluctant to eat a food that he or she never had before, or someone might be reluctant to ride a roller-coaster because it looks scary.
>
> Tell about something you would be reluctant to do. Try to use *reluctant* when you tell about it. You could start by saying something like "I would be reluctant to _____."
>
> What's the word we've been talking about?

Note how the instruction for *reluctant* was presented:

- First, the word was contextualized for its role in the story. (In the story, Lisa was *reluctant* to leave the laundromat without Corduroy.)
- The children were asked to repeat the word so that they could create a phonological representation of the word. (Say the word with me.)
- Next, the meaning of the word was explained. (*Reluctant* means you are not sure you want to do something.)
- Examples in contexts other than the one used in the story were provided. (Someone might be reluctant to eat a food that they never had before, or someone might be reluctant to ride a roller-coaster because it looks scary.)

- Children interacted with examples or provided their own examples. (Tell about something you would be reluctant to do. Try to use *reluctant* when you tell about it. You could start by saying something like "I would be reluctant to _____.")
- Finally, children said the word again to reinforce its phonological representation. (What's the word we've been talking about?)

Vocabulary instruction always began with the context from the story, because it provided a situation that was already familiar to children and provided a rich example of the word's use. However, it is important to move beyond this context in providing and eliciting examples of the word's use. This is not only because multiple contexts are needed for learners to construct a meaningful and memorable representation of the word. It is also important because young children have a very strong tendency to limit a word's use to the context in which it was initially presented.

Consider the following exchange, which took place when a class of kindergarten children were asked to talk about something they might be reluctant to do:

CHILD 1:   I would be reluctant to leave my teddy bear in the laundromat.

TEACHER: Well, that's just like what Lisa did in the story. Try to think about something you might be reluctant to do that is not like Lisa.

CHILD 2:   I would be reluctant to leave my teddy bear in the supermarket.

TEACHER: Okay, that's a little different than what Lisa was reluctant to do, but try to think of something that you would be reluctant to do that is very different than what Lisa was reluctant to do.

CHILD 3:   I would be reluctant to leave my drums at my friend's house.

TEACHER: That's pretty different from what Lisa was reluctant to do, but can we think of something that you would be reluctant to do that isn't about leaving something somewhere.

CHILD 3:   I would be reluctant to change a baby's diaper!

Two of us were present when that exchange occurred, and we both agreed that because of the diaper example most of the children in that class would remember the meaning of *reluctant* with ease!

The tendency to limit a word's use to a single context does not occur only at the earliest levels, however; we have seen this at many grade levels. The most recent was a visit to a fifth-grade class in which the word *desperately* had been introduced through an example of a character desperately looking for car keys. We visited several days after the initial introduction, and when the students were asked to provide examples of *desperately*, every example provided was about desperately looking for something (lunch money, house key, bus pass).

In trying to reduce this tendency, it is very important that examples be provided that are beyond the original context. But notice that even though the instruction for *reluctant* did provide two additional example contexts—being reluctant to eat something and being reluctant to ride something—the children in the above example transcript all went back to the context for *reluctant* that was in the trade book. Thus, in addition to providing other contexts, and often multiple other contexts, teachers need to work with their students, as the one in the foregoing example did, to help them move the word beyond one context or one use.

The Rest of the Activity for *Corduroy*

Below we provide the instructional activities for *insisted* and *drowsy*, the other words from *A Pocket for Corduroy* (Freeman, 1978) singled out for instruction. Notice that the components discussed above are present.

> In the story, Lisa's mother *insisted* that she leave the laundromat when it was closing. *Insisted* means to say that something MUST be done—you won't take no for an answer. Let's say the word aloud.
>
> Your mother might insist that you wear mittens when it is cold outside. She doesn't just TELL you to wear them, she makes sure you have them on before you go out!
>
> - If you were in charge of helping your class get ready to go on a trip, think of something you would insist that everybody do. Try to use the new word when you tell us. You could start out by saying "I would insist that _____."
>
> What's the word we're learning?

In the story, Corduroy felt *drowsy* when he landed in the laundry basket after his adventures in the laundromat. *Drowsy* means feeling as though you are going to fall asleep. Let's all say our word together.

- Sometimes riding in the car makes people feel drowsy, as though they want to take a nap. What might make you feel drowsy, loud drum playing or soft music? Why?
- When might you feel drowsy? In the middle of your favorite TV program or after swimming on a hot day? Why?

What's the word we're learning?

Using All Three Words

After the target words for a story have been presented as described above, there is an activity in which all the words are brought together. In the case at hand, that activity is as follows:

We talked about three words: *insisted, reluctant, drowsy*. Let's think about them.

- Show us how your mother might look if she insisted you go to bed.
- Show us how you would look if you felt reluctant about taking your little sister to the park.
- Show us how you would look if you sat down in a comfortable chair and started to feel drowsy.

TAKING A CLOSER LOOK AT TEACHING WORDS TO YOUNG CHILDREN

When considering the components we identified for developing instruction for vocabulary from trade books, the first one, contextualizing a word for its role in a story, is quite straightforward (e.g., In the story, Lisa was reluctant to leave the laundromat without Corduroy). The second component, developing an explanation, or what we have also called a student-friendly definition, was discussed in Chapter 3. The two features we identified for developing student-friendly definitions—characterizing the word and explaining the meaning in everyday language—hold for young children. The latter is perhaps even more important.

Definitions for Young Children

Below we provide some examples of the kind of language we used to develop student-friendly definitions for young children:

- If something is *dazzling*, that means that it's so bright that you can hardly look at it. After lots of long, gloomy winter days, sunshine on a sunny day might seem dazzling.
- *Strange* describes something different from what you are used to seeing or hearing.
- *Exhausted* means feeling so tired that you can hardly move.
- When people are *amusing*, they are usually funny or they make you happy to watch them. A clown at a circus is amusing.
- When someone is a *nuisance*, he or she is bothering you.

Note that some of the definitions have an example embedded in them. For some words it is particularly hard to describe their meaning in general terms to young children given the limited vocabulary they have. That is, it can be hard to make new words clearly differentiated through words that are understandable to young children. Hence, folding an example into the definition can help to clarify and pinpoint the word's meaning.

Uses of the Word beyond the Story Context

Beyond sometimes folding examples into an initial definition, it is very important to provide examples of the word's use in contexts beyond its use in the story. Creating examples is not always easy. We get started by thinking about places young children are familiar with (e.g., school, home, park, street, playground); things they do (e.g., eat, sleep, play, go to school, watch TV); things they like and are interested in (e.g., animals, food, clothing, toys, books, nature.) Consider the examples we developed for the words defined above:

- For *dazzling*: a big diamond ring; teeth after getting them cleaned at the dentist.
- For *strange*: a dog that meows; a fish that barks.
- For *exhausted*: how someone probably feels after running a long, long race, or after cleaning the house all day.
- For *amusing*: watching animals play at the zoo; seeing someone perform magic tricks.
- For *nuisance*: a baby brother or sister making a mess; someone who keeps interrupting you when you are talking.

ACTIVITIES THAT ENCOURAGE CHILDREN TO INTERACT WITH WORDS

The final activity for each word provides situations in which children have to interact with the target word, often by responding to and explaining examples as well as creating their own examples. As you review the ones below, notice the extent to which children will have to deal with the word's meaning in order to complete the task.

Questions, Reasons, and Examples

- If you are walking around a dark room, you need to do it *cautiously*. Why? What are some other things that need to be done cautiously?
- What is something you could do to *impress* your teacher? Why? What is something you could do that might impress your mother?
- Which of these things might be *extraordinary*? Why or why not?
  —A shirt that was comfortable, or a shirt that washed itself?
  —A flower that kept blooming all year, or a flower that bloomed for 3 days?
  —A person who has a library card, or a person who has read all the books in the library?

Making Choices

- If any of the things I say might be examples of people *clutching* something, say "Clutching." If not, don't say anything.

—Holding on tightly to a purse
—Holding a fistful of money
—Softly petting a cat's fur
—Holding on to branches when climbing a tree
—Blowing bubbles and trying to catch them

- If any of the things I say would make someone look *radiant*, say "You'd be radiant." If not, don't say anything.
  —Winning a million dollars
  —Getting a hug from a favorite movie star
  —Walking to the post office
  —Cleaning your room
  —Having the picture you painted hung up in the school library

- I'll say some things, if they sound *leisurely*, say "Leisurely." If you'd need to be in a hurry, say "Hurry."
  —Taking a walk in the park
  —Firefighters getting to a fire
  —Runners in a race
  —Sitting and talking to friends
  —A dog lying in the sun

USING ALL THE WORDS

As shown earlier in the vocabulary activities for the three words from *A Pocket for Corduroy* (Freeman, 1978), the lesson concludes with a short activity in which all the words that had been considered during that lesson are brought together. Each of these is initiated with a statement something like "We've talked about three words (words are specified). Let's think about them some more."

Relating Words

To develop a concluding activity, a good way to start is to see whether there is anything about the words that is related. In the case of *reluctant*, *insisted*, and *drowsy*, we noticed that each word might be expressed through facial expressions, so that is what was done.

Sentences

Sometimes more than one of the instructed words can be used in a sentence. For example, in the case of *prefer, ferocious*, and *budge*, we could develop the following question:

- Would you *prefer* to *budge* a sleeping lamb or a *ferocious* lion? Why?

Choices

In the case of *pounce, sensible*, and *raucous*, we could ask children to choose between two words:

- If you get your clothes ready to wear to school before you go to sleep, would that be *sensible* or *raucous*?
- If you and your friends were watching a funny TV show together and began to laugh a lot, would you sound *pounce* or *raucous*?

One Context for All the Words

Most of the time, however, it is difficult to find relationships among the target words. What can be done, though, is to use a single context. For example, notice how the words *immense, miserable*, and *leisurely* are used in the questions below:

- What would an *immense* plate of spaghetti look like?
- Why might you feel *miserable* after eating all that spaghetti?
- What would it look like to eat spaghetti in a *leisurely* way?

Same Format

Finally, one can bring some coherence to an activity by using the same format for all three words. Several examples follow:

- If you satisfy your *curiosity*, do you need to find out more or have you found out all that you need? Why?

- If a dog was acting *menacing*, would you want to pet it or move away? Why?
- If you wanted to see something *exquisite*, would you go to a museum or a grocery store? Why?
- Is *imagine* more like dreaming or sneezing? Why?
- Is *snarl* something a fish might do or a lion might do? Why?
- Is *grumpy* a way you might feel or a way you might move? Why?

Children Create Examples

In the last two examples above, the format asked the child to make a choice and to explain the choice. The explanation is the most important part, because it requires the child to explicitly think through how the word fits the choices in the questions in order to express the relationship between the example and the word. Another format we used to prompt children's thinking of how a word fits a context was to have them create examples such as these:

> If there was an *emergency* at an amusement park, what might have happened?

> If you had a friend who watched TV all the time, how might you *coax* him into getting some exercise?

The "Using All the Word" activities we created to conclude a Text Talk lesson were both a way to get another encounter with each word and a way to bring all the words together to begin the process of having them become a natural part of the children's language rather then isolated, specialized items.

• *You Try It* •

Select three words from a children's trade book that you would like to share with your students. Develop activities for students to interact with the words by selecting one or more of the following formats as described on pages 54–57:

- Questions, Reasons, and Examples
- Making Choices

- Using All the Words
  —Relating Words
  —Sentences
  —Choices
  —Children Create Examples

A SAMPLING OF SEVERAL
INSTRUCTIONAL SEQUENCES

Having taken apart the instruction to analyze the processes that the activities are intended to promote, we now put it back together again by provide some complete examples. Our thinking in providing them is that taking a leisurely stroll through several sets of activities may develop a rich mindset for developing such activities. Below are the vocabulary activities from Text Talk that were developed for one story each from kindergarten, first, and second grades.

Doctor DeSoto (Steig, 1982) was a favorite among the kindergarten classes in which we worked. Doctor DeSoto is a dentist who happens to be a mouse. Although he usually refuses to treat dangerous animals, he and his dental-assistant wife take pity on a fox suffering from a toothache. After being treated, the fox decides to eat them, but the DeSotos outwit him by creating a concoction that makes his jaws stick together. The words from the story that we chose to deal with after the story had been read and discussed are *timid, morsel,* and *protect.* Following is the instruction that was developed.

In the story, it said that the DeSotos wouldn't even treat a *timid* cat. *Timid* means "shy, maybe a little scared." Let's say the word together.

People can be timid, too. For example, if you walked into a big room full of people you didn't know you might feel a little timid.

- Show how you would look if you felt timid.
- Show how a timid cat might act.

Let's say the word together.

In the story, the fox thought of Dr. DeSoto as a tasty *morsel*. A morsel is a very small piece of food. Let's say the word together.

The fox thought of Dr. DeSoto as a morsel of food because in comparison to a fox a mouse is very tiny.

If the food that I name is a very small piece of food, say "Morsel." If it isn't a morsel, don't say anything

- One Cheerio
- A whole pie
- A raisin
- A turkey dinner
- A cake crumb

Let's say the word together.

In the story, Dr. and Mrs. DeSoto had to come up with a plan to *protect* themselves. *Protect* means "to keep something safe." Let's say the word together. You protect your feet from getting wet by wearing boots. A mother cat protects her kittens by keeping them close to her.

I'll say some things, and you tell me how they could protect you

- A pot holder
- A smoke alarm
- Mittens
- Seat belts

What word are we learning?

Let's think about all three words: *morsel, timid,* and *protect.*

- If a little boy walked out on a stage and saw a lot of people in the audience, would he feel *timid* or *morsel*?
- Would someone wrap a baby in a warm blanket to *protect* him or *timid* him?
- Is a morsel more like a slice of cake or a crumb of cake?

Beware of the Bears (MacDonald, 1999) was a very popular book in first grade. Goldilocks and the three bears from the well-known story are the main characters in this tale. The bears, angry about the fact that Goldilocks made herself at home at their place, decide to follow her and behave in the same bad-mannered way in her home. They have a grand time, sampling different types of cereals, trying out all of the bathroom products, and the like. They have a pillow fight which is interrupted by Goldilocks, who informs them that this is not her house but the wolf's house. The words selected for this story were *launch*, *gleeful*, and *astonished*.

In the story when the bears were playing and throwing the cereal around, Daddy Bear *launched* some spoonfuls of cereal in the air. *Launch* means to toss or move something upward fast. Say the word.

If what I say could be launched, say "That could be launched." If you think they are not things that could be launched, say "No way."

- A rocket
- An elephant
- A paper airplane
- A tree
- Some fireworks

What's our word?

In the story, the bears watched for Goldilocks's reactions *gleefully*. That means they were very happy about the way she was going to find her house a mess. *Gleeful* means "so happy that you feel a little silly or giggly." Say our word.

Which would make you feel gleeful—so happy you might want to giggle?

- A party in school or extra work to do for homework?
- A trip to an amusement park or a trip to the dentist?
- Having your best friend move away or having them stay over for the whole weekend?
- Staying home from school because you're sick or because of a big snowstorm?

What's the word we are learning?

In the story, the bears were *astonished* when Goldilocks started laughing at the big mess they'd made. That means that the bears were very surprised that the mess would make her laugh—because they thought it was *her* house. If something makes you astonished, that means it is so unusual that you are surprised and shocked by it. Say our word.

Would you be astonished if—

- You met someone from Cleveland or from the planet Venus?
- Your dog said hello or your baby cousin said hello?
- Your mother served spaghetti for dinner or if she served a big banana split?

What is something you might be astonished to see in the sky? Start your sentence with "I'd be astonished. . . . "

We talked about three words: *launched, gleeful,* and *astonished.* Let's think about them some more.

- Which would you more likely want to *launch*—a kite or a car?
- If your teacher was making you feel *gleeful,* what would he or she probably be doing or telling you?
- What would make you more *astonished*—to find a dinosaur bone or a bird's bone?

We used *Chestnut Cove* (Eagan, 1995) in the second grade. It's about a town called Chestnut Cove where people take the time to really enjoy life and help one another when needed. Then the king offers his kingdom to the person who grows the best watermelon, and everyone gets greedy. The citizens begin to tend to their gardens and stop being nice to each other. The need to rescue a pig causes the citizens to realize that the contest was destroying their town, and they decide to have a picnic and eat all of the watermelons. The next day the king came and declared the watermelons "disappointing." But the citizens were very satisfied. The words selected were *entire, incredible,* and *emotion.*

In the story the king said that the winner of the contest would get his *entire* kingdom. That means that person would get the whole thing, all of it. Let's say the word.

Let's think about what *entire* means.

- If I said the entire class is here—what does that mean?
- If I said the rug covers the entire room—what does that mean?
- If it rained for your entire vacation—what does that mean?

Now see if you can say a sentence to answer my question about *entire*.

- How would you feel if you ate an entire cake yourself? (Encourage children to begin "If I ate an entire cake. . . . ")
- How would you feel if you ran the entire way to school? (Encourage children to begin "If I ran the entire way. . . . ")

What's our word?

In the story, when the king came to Chestnut Cove, he made an *incredible* announcement, saying that the person who could grow the biggest watermelon could have all his riches. *Incredible* means "unbelievable." Let's say the word.

Sometimes people might tell you things that sound incredible. That means it's hard to believe that it's true.

Which would be incredible?

- A cow that can fly or a cow that eats grass?
- A talking teacher or a talking horse?
- First graders driving their own bus to school or first graders riding a school bus?
- Finding a live dinosaur or finding dinosaur bones?

Has something incredible ever happened to you? Maybe it was something so good or so lucky that it felt incredible. Tell us about it. Try to use *incredible* when you're telling us about it. You might start by saying something like, "Here's something incredible that happened to me. . . . "

What's our word?

In the story, when everyone rescued Mrs. Lark's pig Eloise, her eyes were filled with *emotion*. That means she was feeling things deeply and maybe she wanted to cry because she was so thankful for people's help. Let's say the word.

We all have a lot of emotions—we laugh and cry and get angry and scared. All our feelings are called emotions.

When different things happen, we feel different emotions, like some things make us feel happy and loving, others sad, or disappointed, or angry. I'll name some situations, and you tell me what emotion you might feel if it happened to you.

- Learning that your best friend can stay with you all weekend
- Losing a pet
- Getting a big hug from your grandmother
- Hearing that a big storm is coming when you're alone at home

What's our word?

We talked about *entire*, *incredible*, and *emotion*. Let's think about those words some more.

- Which is more *incredible*—a plane landing at the airport or a plane landing on the school yard?
- On Saturdays, what is your favorite way to spend the *entire* day?
- If you watch a football game and at first your team is winning and then they lose—what kinds of *emotions* do you feel?

▪ You Try It ▪

The sections above have presented principles and examples for teaching young children useful, interesting, and sophisticated words. The basic instructional sequence is as follows:

1. Read the story.
2. Contextualize the word within the story.
3. Have children say the word.
4. Provide a student-friendly explanation of the word.

5. Present examples of the word used in contexts different from the story context.
6. Engage children activities that get them to interact with the words.
7. Have children say the word.

Select a story that you would like to share with young children. Choose three words from the story. Design activities for one of the words using the instructional sequence described above.

THE TEACHER'S ROLE IN SUPPORTING CHILDREN'S LEARNING

An important element for developing children's understanding of word meanings is the teacher's reinforcement of those nascent understandings. Especially for young children it is important that the teacher give voice to the elements of developing word meaning that may be difficult for children to express on their own. And it is equally important that the teacher reveal aspects of word meaning that may not be readily apparent to young learners. No matter how well planned a lesson may be, a major part of all teaching is that combination of thoughtfulness and improvisational skill that allows a teacher to respond productively to children's comments. In this section, we provide some of the ways teachers responded to what children said to enhance children's understanding as well to encourage them to respond to comments offered by their peers.

Reinforcing Connections between Words and Meanings

When children contribute examples, it is important to acknowledge the appropriateness of the example and to show how it connect to elements of the word's meaning. For example:

TEACHER: Who can tell about something that would be *absurd*?

CHILD: A rock that can walk.

TEACHER: A rock that can walk would really be absurd, because that doesn't make any sense at all!

TEACHER: How might you *rescue* a cat that was stuck high up in a tree?

CHILD: Once my cat was up in a tree and I climbed up.

TEACHER: You climbed the tree—that would be a good way to rescue the cat.

TEACHER: Tell us about something that would be a *feast*.

CHILD: Taking a picnic to the park.

TEACHER: Sure, a picnic at a park could be a feast, because you might bring lots of different kinds of food—chicken, potato salad, sandwiches, pie.

TEACHER: What is something you might *gaze* at on a hot day?

CHILD: I'd gaze at a swimming pool.

TEACHER: Okay. If it's a hot day you might gaze at that swimming pool, because what would you really want to do?

Adding to Children's Network of Related Words

Asking children how a new word relates to words they already know helps them understand how words fit into their previous knowledge and gives them ideas of how they can use the new word. For example:

TEACHER: When you're *exhausted* you're really tired, tell us how it feels?

CHILD: Sweaty.

CHILD: Like I want to lay down.

CHILD: Out of breath.

TEACHER: If somebody is *grumpy*, how are they acting, what do they do?

CHILD: Mad.

CHILD: Got a mean face.

CHILD: Being ugly.

Suggesting Ways to Apply the Word

Prompting children to think about situations in their lives that relate to a new word increases the chances that children will recall and use the word when appropriate circumstances occur. Some examples follow:

> TEACHER: When you come in from recess, you could say "I'm *exhausted*." When you climb the stairs, you could say, "I'm exhausted." When else could you say you were exhausted?
>
> CHILD: After riding my bike.
>
> CHILD: When I stay up late.
>
> CHILD: When I run to see who wins.

> TEACHER: I need to *remind* myself to stop at the store on the way home from school. Sometimes I remind you to bring in your homework. When are some times you might have to remind someone to do something?
>
> CHILD: Remind my mother to help me plant seeds tomorrow.
>
> CHILD: Remind my brother it's my turn to say the [TV] program to watch.

Getting Children Involved in Responding to Peers' Comments

In many cases, connections between children's examples and word meaning can be provided by the children themselves. Prompting children to do this helps them develop the kind of thinking that promotes the building of such connections. Having other children play this role also spreads around the thinking by getting several children involved. And, further, it makes it more likely that children will attend to their peers' examples if they know they might be asked to comment on them. After a child offers an example of how a word might be used, a teacher might follow up by posing questions such as those below, to elicit comments from other students:

- Does what Jack just told us about sound *festive* to you?
- What do you think of that—could a new bike be *dazzling*?
- What does it mean that Shana is *reluctant* to eat spinach?"

MAINTAINING WORDS

The vocabulary research strongly points to the need for frequent encounters with new words if they are to become a permanent part of an individual's vocabulary repertoire. In Text Talk, target words were placed on a bulletin board next to the cover of the story from which they came. Tally marks were placed next to words when they were mentioned by the teacher or children. In this way, a class's "favorite words" were identified. There are many variations of this notion, which are discussed in Chapter 7.

There are other ways to keep children thinking about and using target words. Some that we observed are included in the following subsections.

Applying Learned Words to New Stories

Both teachers and children often noticed when words they had learned appeared in subsequent stories that were read. But we also noticed occasions when a learned word did not necessarily appear in a story but could be applied. In these cases, teachers challenged children to apply vocabulary words from past stories to the one being read. An example of this situation occurred during a reading of *Curious George Goes to a Chocolate Factory* (Rey & Rey, 1998). In that story, George, the curious monkey, loves chocolate and nearly causes disruption in a chocolate factory by trying to find his favorite candy. But he ends up helping in an unintended way, and he is rewarded with a free box of chocolates for his efforts. The teacher asked the following questions that relate words learned from previous stories to the Curious George story:

- We learned some words in other stories that could fit here, too. How about the word *craving*? How does that describe something that happened in this story?
- Remember the word *deserve*? George got a box of chocolates as a

present at the end. Do you think that he deserved to get that?
Why?
- Does anybody remember a word that George might use to talk
  about the candy? It's a word we used to talk about the things the
  wolf baked for the chickens in *The Wolf's Chicken Stew* (Kasza,
  1987). He thought the candy was _____ [*scrumptious*].

Using Words in Reading and Writing Situations

Teachers developed a number of different ways to use the words children were learning in various reading and writing situations, including
the following:

- Incorporating the words in the daily message.
- For example: Today is Tuesday. It is a *lovely* day outside. The sun
  is *radiant*. I *insist* that we work hard this morning so we can all go
  outside at recess.
- Creating a dictionary with word meanings and sample sentences.
- Encouraging children to use the words in their writing.
- Writing words on slips of paper and placing them into a container,
  and when there is some downtime in the day, such as just before
  lunch, challenging children to create sentences with that word.

IN SUMMARY

This chapter has focused on an instructional sequence to enrich the listening and speaking vocabularies of young children. The words come
from the sophisticated language found in children's trade books, which
teachers share with children by reading them aloud, or from labeling
ideas in the simplest stories with sophisticated words. The vocabulary
selected for teaching meet the criteria for Tier Two words of importance
and utility, instructional potential, and conceptual understanding. That
is, the words are ones that children will be able to use in many contexts;
the words can be used in a variety of instructional activities; and the concepts to which the words refer are within the intellectual grasp of the
children.

▪ *Your Turn* ▪

We invite you to use what you have learned in this chapter to create some lesson plans for a week of vocabulary instruction. Select a book that you would like to share with the children. Decide which words you would like the children to learn. After the story has been read—which may or may not be on the same day—provide explanations of the words in context and create activities in which children have to engage with the meanings of the words.

CHAPTER 5

Developing Vocabulary in the Later Grades

Ryan, Julie, and Andrew gather in a corner of their classroom to complete work on a group project. Ryan pantomimes stretching in his seat, and then, grinning, grabs Julie's pencil out of her hand.

JULIE: It baffles me why you're such a buffoon.

RYAN: Oh, don't be so antagonistic.

ANDREW: Cut out the bantering, you two. We have work to do here.

When effective instruction is part of classroom practice and students are encouraged to use the sophisticated words they are learning, they begin to take true ownership of the words that are presented. Their ownership can be seen in the ease with which they can use the words in everyday exchanges. Even trading insults takes on a new character! The purpose of this chapter is to describe the kind of instruction that inspires and supports word ownership by students in the upper elementary grades, middle school, and high school.

FREQUENT, RICH, AND EXTENDED INSTRUCTION

In this chapter, we focus on effective vocabulary instruction after words have been introduced. First, we provide a general overview of what we call frequent, rich, and extended instruction. Then, we provide examples of such instruction with lesson sequences for specific sets of words for students in the upper elementary grades, middle school, and high school.

One of the strongest findings about vocabulary instruction, whether direct instruction or learning words from context, is that multiple encounters are required before a word is really known (e.g., Stahl & Fairbanks, 1986), that is, if it is to affect a student's comprehension and become a useful and permanent part of the student's vocabulary repertoire. So, the vocabulary instruction discussed in this chapter is toward that end. The design of the instruction and many of the examples used come from our earlier vocabulary studies (e.g., Beck et al., 1982; McKeown et al., 1983, 1985).

In our vocabulary research, the instruction we provided was designed around three features:

1. Frequent encounters with the words
2. Richness of instruction
3. Extension of word use beyond the classroom

Frequency

Our basic design was to introduce about 10 words per week and present activities around the words daily. By the end of the week, each word had often been the focus of attention (some 8–10 times). We also included words from previous weeks in the activities so that those words would be maintained.

Richness

By "rich" instruction, we mean instruction that goes beyond definitional information to get students actively involved in using and thinking about word meanings and creating lots of associations among words. The instructional activities varied widely, but the pattern was similar each week. We began with the kind of word introduction described in Chapter 3 that involved discussion around a student-friendly explanation. Students had log sheets of the words and their meanings that they kept in a vocabulary notebook.

Throughout the rest of the week, we made sure to provide opportunities for students to:

- Use the words.
- Explore facets of word meaning.
- Consider relationships among words.

Students' Use of Words

Having students create uses for words was important to ensure that the word was an active part of their vocabularies. If students did not know how to create a context around a word, then the word would become just an isolated piece of information. Engaging students in talking about situations a word would describe or in considering instances when the word would be an appropriate choice was an important way to make sure that the word became part of a network of ideas.

Facets of Word Meaning

Students were asked to respond to various characteristics of the words to help them see a word not as a single block of meaning but as having different facets to its meaning. The purpose was to make students' word knowledge flexible so that they could both understand the word and apply the word to a variety of contexts. If a student's understanding of a word is limited to a narrow definition or stereotypical contexts (e.g., *delighted* is always used in association with receiving a gift), then many applications of the word will not be comprehensible and the student will have only limited opportunities to use the word in speech and writing.

One way we commonly used to reveal facets of meaning was an activity in which students were asked to differentiate between two descriptions by labeling them as an example or a nonexample of the target word. The descriptions were quite similar, differing only in features that were critical to the word's meaning. For example:

banter

A husband and wife argue about what to have for dinner.	A husband and wife kid each other about who ate more at dinner.

impatient

A boy tells his friends about his birthday party and hopes they can come.	A boy counts the days until his birthday and wishes the time would go faster.

retort

The player comes back with a quick answer after the referee calls a foul on him.	The player complains to the coach after the referee calls a foul on him.

glum

The class decides to have a party indoors when they learn that the picnic has been rained out.	The class learns that the picnic has been rained out and they have to do work instead.

berate

A police officer yells at a driver whose car is blocking traffic.	A police officer calls a tow truck to move a car that is blocking traffic.

Relationships among Words

As a way of moving words beyond narrow associations, we designed activities around relationships among words. In one activity, we presented questions that juxtaposed two target words, such as "Could a *virtuoso* be a *rival*?" In pairing words that were not obviously related, the purpose was to make students pause and really consider whether a relationship existed. One student began to answer the virtuoso/rival question, saying: "No, because a virtuoso is somebody who is good at music and a rival—" He stopped in midsentence, and then continued with some excitement about his insight—"Oh! Yeah, it could be somebody who was good at music who was trying to be better than somebody else who was good at music!" So, suddenly this student saw the words not as straight, closed roads but as intersecting paths from which more complex ideas could be created.

Relationships are also very important because of the way individuals' word knowledge is stored in networks of connected ideas. Thus, the more connections that can be built, the more opportunities there are for an individual to "get to" the knowledge. That means that the chances become greater and greater that words met will set off associations in the network and allow the learner to derive meaning from the contexts in which a word is used.

Additional Features:
Alternative Definitions and Time Constraints

Two other features also characterized what we call rich instruction. These were opportunities to interact with alternative definitions and to respond to words under time constraints.

Definitions for target words appeared several times during each week, and for each appearance we altered the definition somewhat. This was done so that students were not simply memorizing the definition but had to process the description of the word in a meaningful way. Thus, students were truly learning the concepts represented by the words rather than the mere wording of a definition. Here are examples of the definitions used over the course of a week's sequence for two target words:

ambitious

1. Really wanting to succeed in becoming rich or important.
2. Wanting to get ahead by becoming powerful.
3. Wants great success in life.

stern

1. Being very strict about how you look and what you do.
2. Very demanding about how you and others behave.
3. Acts hard and serious.

Activities that were done under time constraints were included to help students develop rapid responses to the meanings of the words so that when the students met the words in a context—in a stream of speech or print—they would be accustomed to accessing the words' meanings quickly. In an activity called "Beat the Clock," students were given one and a half minutes to complete 14 items. Their score was the number of items completed, minus any errors. Here are some sample items:

- *Shrill* sounds can hurt your ears.
    true   false
- *Gregarious* people would rather be alone.
    true   false
- It might be hard to have a conversation where there's a *commotion*.
    true   false
- *Frank* people keep their thoughts to themselves.
    true   false

Beyond the Classroom

In addition to classroom activities, a component of our vocabulary program challenged students to take their word learning outside the classroom. We set up a system called Word Wizard, in which students gained points by bringing in evidence of hearing, seeing, or using target words outside the classroom. We did this not only to enliven the word environment but also because we realized that if students saw vocabulary learning as only a classroom exercise, they were unlikely to develop the kind of understanding about the words that would really enhance their literacy. The Word Wizard activity was highly successful—so much so that it took on a life of its own. We will discuss that activity and other related ones in Chapter 7, which focuses on creating a rich verbal environment.

When instruction is rich, frequent, and extends beyond the lesson and the classroom, we think of it as robust. That is, there is an energy and liveliness to it that pervades the classroom atmosphere. And its effects are clear and powerful. In the next section, we discuss the kinds of results we obtained from the rich, frequent, and extended instruction in our vocabulary research.

RESULTS OF FREQUENT, RICH, EXTENDED INSTRUCTION

What were students able to do after receiving frequent, rich, and extended instruction? Over the course of our vocabulary research, we compared a group of students who had received rich instruction to two other groups of students: one group who had not been instructed, and another group who had received traditional, definition-based instruction. We also compared the effects of less frequent with more frequent encounters.

We examined students' learning on a variety of measures, and the pattern of results was that students who received rich, frequent instruction did better on a variety of measures. They were able to respond more quickly to word meanings in a timed task, and they showed better comprehension of stories containing the target words. In a final rather complex task, context interpretation, students who received rich instruction performed especially better than those who did not. In the context interpretation task, students respond to questions about sentences in which a target word was not used in typical ways. As such, the sentences and questions were constructed to require some complex thinking, let alone knowledge of the word being assessed. For example, students were shown this sentence: "After the prize winners were announced, Stacy ran up to console Meg." Then they were asked, "How do you think Meg had done in the contest?" Since the context invites the notion of congratulations, students then had to reason that if Stacy was consoling Meg, Meg must not have done very well.

Students who had participated in rich instruction were quite successful on this task. Students who had participated in the definition-based instruction, however, were less successful. They often responded to the questions by giving the definition of the word. So, in some sense they "knew" the word, but that knowledge did not help them where it counted. That is, they could not use it to bring meaning to a context. This seemed a particularly compelling result, because what literate people most often need to do with words is use them, not present definitions of them.

Beyond the results from the assessments, our observations in the classrooms demonstrated some other processes at work in these word-rich environments. Specifically, we noticed what we came to call "word ownership" in the students. They knew the words well, and used them easily and appropriately. They also reacted to uses of the words with relish and took obvious pleasure and pride in using them themselves. Another characteristic we noticed developing in the students was "word awareness." That is, not only were the students aware of target words that appeared in their environment, but they also began to take notice of words in a more general way. Students even began drawing our attention to words that they thought we should have included in the program!

The discussion so far in this chapter has presented a generalized picture of purposes and activities that are appropriate for vocabulary development across grade levels from intermediate grades through high school. In the rest of this chapter, we present sequences of vocabulary activities for sets of words at three different levels: upper elementary, middle school, and high school.

UPPER ELEMENTARY GRADES EXAMPLE

We begin by presenting the activities for one set of words from the vocabulary program we created for our research. The program was implemented in fourth-grade classrooms in a small urban public school district. The instruction was arranged in 5-day cycles; the words were presented over 4 days, and on day 5 the students' knowledge of the words was assessed. We should note here that there is nothing magic about a 5-day cycle. Depending on how many words are being presented and the learning goal, less than a 5-day cycle and indeed more than a 5-day cycle can be appropriate. It is important, however, that attention be given to words on at least 2 days, so that there is some follow-up to simply introducing words. Our vocabulary program presented sets of words that were organized around themes. The reason for using themes was that we thought it would help students remember the words by giving them ready-made connections. We also thought that drawing on the themes might well help us in creating more coherent activities.

The theme of words for the example presented here was "How we use our eyes." The target words were *gape, squint, spectator, focus, scrutinize, glimpse, inspector,* and *binoculars*.

Day 1

On the first day the words were introduced using a set of pictures that illustrated each word. The teacher questioned the students about each picture in a way that elicited the meaning elements for the words and then presented a definition based on those elements. Students filled in the definitions on their log sheets. The words were then reviewed by having the students match each word with its picture. Here are the words and the initial definitions:

Target words	Definitions
gape	to stare with your eyes and mouth wide open
spectator	a person who just watches something happen
binoculars	a special kind of glasses for making far away things seem close
squint	to partly close your eyes
focus	to make it easier to see clearly
scrutinize	to look at something very carefully in order to understand it better
glimpse	to catch a quick look
inspector	a person whose job is to check things

Days 2–4

The day after the above words had been introduced, instruction began with a sentence completion activity. The sentence stems, which appear below, were on students' log sheets. The activity was done together with the class. Students offered suggestions to complete a sentence, and through discussion a sentence was developed. Students wrote the agreed-upon sentence completion on their log sheets. The reason for having all students use the same sentence was to ensure that their log sheets had a strong example sentence as a permanent record. Below are the sentence stems for the "eyes" words:

- *gape*
  Mom said I must have been really surprised at my birthday party because I _____.
- *spectator*
  The teacher asked who wanted to be in the class play, but I said I didn't want to act in it, I just _____.
- *binoculars*
  The bird singing up in the tree is too far away for me to see, so _____.

- *squint*
  As I looked at the blackbird, the sunlight from the window got in my eyes, and it _____.
- *focus*
  At first I thought the snowman was a real person, until I _____

  _____.
- *scrutinize*
  I wasn't sure if those were freckles or measles I saw on my friend's face, so _____.
- *glimpse*
  Dad asked me if I knew who the person on the roller-coaster was, but _____.
- *inspector*
  Before the airplane could be cleared for take-off, the _____

  _____.

Another activity that was included on the second day asked students to choose between pairs of target words in responding to questions such as "Which would you do if you had trouble seeing clearly?" [*focus* or *gape*] We implemented the activity as a game with two teams. The teacher began by reading a story that ended with two characters challenging each other as to which had the "fastest eyes in the west." Each team represented one of the characters. For each question, the teacher wrote two words on the board, one under each character's name. The teams then had to applaud if the correct word was posted under their character's name. Here are the items for that activity:

focus   *gape*
- Which would you probably do if you had trouble seeing clearly?

inspector   *spectator*
- What would you probably call every person watching a football game?

squint   *gape*
- Which would you probably do if you needed to wear glasses but didn't have any?

glimpse   *scrutinize*
- Which can you do more quickly?

gape   *scrutinize*
- Which would you probably do if you wanted to concentrate *very* hard on understanding something?

gape   *squint*
- Which would you probably do if some dust blew in your eyes?

spectator   *inspector*
- Who would probably be careful when checking things to make sure they were done right?

binoculars   *spectator*
- Which could you use to help you see where a baseball landed when a home run was hit?

focus   *glimpse*
- Which would you probably do if you couldn't see clearly out of your binoculars?

About midway through a cycle of words, students had to select the target word that fit into a closed sentence. This activity often included words from previous sets, which are marked with an asterisk below. Here are the sentences from the activity sheet:

- The accomplice* wiped away the burglar's fingerprints before the police came, so the _____ couldn't find any clues to the crime. [*inspector*]
- The photographs I took always came out fuzzy until I learned how to _____ the camera. [*focus*]
- I wanted to find out which tree my kite got stuck in, but my friend seized* my _____ before I could look through them. [*binoculars*]
- That virtuoso* must have trouble seeing because she always _____ when she looks at the music. [*squirts*]
- I wasn't sure if the strange-looking vegetable on my plate was edible*, so I _____ it until I figured out what it was. [*scrutinized*]
- When my father came home dressed like a bunny rabbit, I really _____ at him! [*gaped*]
- My brother is going to lead the band in the parade. But I'm just going to watch and be a _____. [*spectator*]

Toward the end of an instructional cycle, there was often an activity that focused on how pairs of words were both alike and different. Students had to choose two words that fit descriptions such as "They're both things you do with your eyes that change the way your face looks. One makes you open your eyes wider than normal; the other makes you close them partly." [*gape* and *squint*] When the activity was completed, the class reviewed the answers together. Here are the rest of the items for the activity:

- They're both people who use their eyes in special ways. One watches something for fun; the other one checks things for a living. [*spectator/inspector*]
- They both have to do with food. With one, you eat a lot; with the other, you stay away from eating food. [*devour/fast*]
- They both have to do with seeing something. With one, you get so quick a look that you might not be sure of what you are seeing; with the other, you look very carefully to make yourself sure. [*glimpse/scrutinize*]
- They both have to do with taking hold of someone or something. With one, you hold someone lovingly; with the other, you grab suddenly. [*embrace/seize*]

The last instructional activity—the one before the next day's assessment—was a timed activity called "Ready, Set, Go." It consisted of four activity sheets, or "laps," which students completed as a partner timed them. Each sheet listed the words on one side and the definitions on the other, and the students had to match them by drawing lines to connect each word and definition. The order of the words for each lap was changed, and the wording of the definitions was altered a little to ensure that students were not just associating specific words with a target word. The goal was to see if one could get faster across the laps.

Day 5

At the end of our cycle of instruction, which in our case was on the fifth day, we assessed students' knowledge of the target words through a multiple-choice test. It is important to keep in mind that when we implemented our vocabulary instruction, we were engaged in a research project that looked at what students had learned in various ways. After each cycle of instruction the assessment we used was a multiple-choice test. However, at the completion of the 12-week intervention, we assessed vocabulary understanding at deeper levels. Below we provide the multiple-choice test for the "eyes" theme. Then we discuss some general issues about assessment and provide some examples of assessments that are deeper than the multiple-choice test.

Note that in the items for the "eyes" words, each of the distracters—the incorrect choices—was related to the week's theme, and the correct response was a wording of the definition different from the ones that students had worked with. Thus, it provided a moderately challenging assessment of their knowledge.

- *squint*
  - to give a mean look
  - to pretend you are asleep
  - to partly shut your eyes
  - to look down at your feet
- *focus*
  - to make more clear
  - to bother by staring at
  - to look at dreamily
  - to use glasses for reading
- *gape*
  - to blink several times in a row
  - to look wide-eyed and openmouthed
  - to roll your eyes
  - to raise your eyebrows
- *glimpse*
  - to take a picture of
  - to get only a peek
  - to shut your eyes tightly
  - to look hurt
- *spectator*
  - a person who is good at playing games
  - someone who doesn't pay very good attention
  - a person who can't see very well
  - someone who is watching something

- *binoculars*

  a toy for looking at cartoon cards

  a special thing used by doctors to test your eyes

  special glasses for seeing far away

  a mask to keep you from seeing
- *scrutinize*

  look ashamed

  try to remember what you see on a page

  look cross-eyed

  look carefully and closely
- *inspector*

  someone who has a job checking things

  a person who makes glasses

  an eye doctor

  a person who teaches blind people

WHAT'S DIFFERENT FOR MIDDLE SCHOOL AND HIGH SCHOOL STUDENTS?

Vocabulary work in middle school and high school should allow deeper explorations of language—how language gives meaning and how words mean what they mean. This kind of approach makes an especially stark contrast to vocabulary as synonyms. Teaching new words as synonyms for known words is a common way to present vocabulary to students, perhaps particularly so for students at middle schools and high schools where often the goal is to prepare their students for various standardized tests. But the synonym approach, although handy for providing a quick anchor point for a word, is a bankrupt way to teach word meaning. Building understanding of language comes through developing knowledge of both the similarities and the differences among words and the precise roles they can play. A focus here is on exploration of complex dimensions of a word's meaning and the relationships that exist to other words along some of those dimensions—how the word may be related to others through some components but not others.

The vocabulary work at upper grade levels can also be more rooted to a text and dealt with in a way that both teaches the words and brings enriched understanding to the text. It can bring attention to how authors use words, the deliberateness with which an author chooses a specific word, and thus what role it plays in what the author is communicating. These kinds of things can indeed be done with younger students, but there can be a more rigorous focus with older students.

MIDDLE SCHOOL EXAMPLE

The example we provide is based on an excerpt from Mark Twain's *The Prince and the Pauper* (1881/1992), the story of Tom, a young pauper who switches identity with a prince and is subsequently crowned king. The text is rich in language, offering abundant possibilities for vocabulary work. In the segment of the story we use for this example, it is Tom's second day as king, and he is faced with determining the fate of a man who has been accused of poisoning someone.

We have selected ten target words. None is really crucial to understanding the story, but several embody the theme of the selection. *Compassion* most captures the theme of the segment. *Homage* and *imperious* tie in with Tom's present royal situation, and *indecorum* is a source of concern for Tom in his present role. The other words could be of help in local comprehension, potentially playing a role in understanding a specific sentence or so. To provide a flavor of the story and its language, we present the context in which each word appears in the story here:

- Tom said the words which Lord Hertford, who had become his friend, put into his mouth from time to time, but he was too new to such things, and too ill at ease to accomplish more than *tolerable* success.
- He looked *sufficiently* like a king, but he was ill able to feel like one.
- But there was a lifting of his cloud in one way—he felt less uncomfortable than at first; he was getting a little used to his circumstances and surroundings . . . he found that the presence and *homage* of the great and afflicted embarrassed him less and less sharply with every hour that drifted over his head.
- In truth, being a king is not all dreariness—it hath its *compensations* and conveniences.
- Death—and a violent death—for this poor unfortunate! The

thought wrung Tom's heartstrings. The spirit of *compassion* took control of him, to the exclusion of all other considerations.

- His concern made him even forget, for the moment, that he was but the false shadow of a king, not the substance. Before he knew it he had *blurted* out the command.
- Then he blushed scarlet, and a sort of apology sprung to his lips; but observing that his order had wrought no sort of surprise in the earl or the waiting page, he *suppressed* the words he was about to utter.
- The earl's face showed *profound* gratification, for he was a man of merciful and generous impulses—a thing not very common with his class in that fierce age.
- Another blush followed this unregal outburst, and he covered his *indecorum* as well as he could by adding, "It enraged me that a man should be hanged upon such idle, hare-brained evidence!"
- How sanely he put his questions. How like his former natural self was this abrupt, *imperious* disposal of the matter!

Here are the definitions that we developed for the words:

Target words	Definition
tolerable	just barely good enough, but not of high quality
sufficient[ly]	enough of something for a certain purpose
homage	great respect and honor toward someone, usually someone in authority
compensation[s]	something done to balance or make up for something else (it can be a payment for work done, or something good that happens to make up for something bad)
compassion	a feeling of sympathy for someone who is suffering and a desire to help them
blurt[ed]	to say something suddenly that you might have held in if you had thought about it
suppress[ed]	to hold back from doing or saying something because you think it shouldn't be said or done

profound	describes a feeling that is deeply felt or believed
indecorum	behavior that is not acceptable for the situation
imperious	describes behavior in which someone commands others to follow

At this point, we will assume that the words and definitions have been introduced and the story read. We now pick up on what we would do with the words to further develop students' knowledge and understanding of them.

Record the Words

It is useful for students to keep a written record (e.g., a vocabulary notebook or journal) of words that are introduced. Students should add the words and definitions to whatever ongoing records are being used for vocabulary in the classroom. An example of the use of each word should also be added to the record, and the focus of one activity—to be done later—can be to develop examples for the vocabulary record. This activity would come a bit later to give students a chance to get to know the words first. In that way, students will be able to create more meaningful examples.

Facets of Word Meanings

Use the context of the story as a basis for discussing the words. Talking about their applications in the story can prompt students to explore and elaborate on the meanings. This deepens their understanding of the words and helps to build connections to other words and concepts they know.

The discussion could begin by asking which of the words best characterizes what the story is all about. *Compassion* is the most likely answer, although any candidates that can be defended are possible. When a candidate is offered, reasons for why that captures the story line should follow.

Here are discussion starters for the rest of the words:

- What might Tom have considered to be *compensations* for his present state?
- *Imperious* is often appropriate for describing a king—How appropriate is it to Tom?
- How do Tom's *blurting* out and *suppressing* his words relate to a judgment of him as imperious?
- What made Tom think he looked *sufficiently* like a king? Do you agree?
- Tom was afraid that he showed *indecorum* by sparing the prisoner's life. Why was that indecorum? Do you think Tom showed indecorum in his dealing with the prisoner?
- Who was paying *homage* to whom in the story? In what ways can it be said that: Tom paid homage to the prisoner; the earl paid homage to Tom; those around Tom paid homage to him as king?
- When Tom decided that the prisoner should not be boiled in oil, the earl's face showed *profound* gratification. What other profound feelings are shown in the story?
- Do you think that Tom showed *tolerable* success as king in this episode? Is *tolerable* an appropriate way to describe it?

Relationships among Words

The activity below pairs words so that students have to consider how meanings interact in order to respond to the questions.

- Would you pay homage to something tolerable?
- Would you have compassion for someone imperious?
- Would you suppress a profound thought?
- Would blurting out your thoughts be an example of indecorum?
- When would compensation not be sufficient?

Most of the questions are set up for yes or no answers, and although one response is more likely, either is acceptable if it can be justified. The point of the activity is for students to decide how they would respond and then support their response. For example, "Would you pay homage to something tolerable?" could be answered:

- No, if something was tolerable—like just okay, but not really very good—I wouldn't give it homage, or respect it.
- Yes, I might, if something was tolerable and all the other choices were not even tolerable. Then something tolerable could deserve homage.

Students' Use of Words

This activity was designed to give students practice in using the words, and it doubles as a way to create examples for the vocabulary record. Divide students into groups and have each group develop a sentence for several of the words. Students should strive to make the meaning of the word clear within the sentence. After sentences are developed, have them shared with the class and edited as desired or necessary. This will ensure that the examples are strong and appropriate, and optimally helpful for demonstrating word meanings.

Beyond the Classroom

Give students the assignment of watching the TV news one night to see how many of the target words could be used to describe things that are reported. News reports often have stories of compassion or indecorum; examples of imperious behavior might not be too hard to come up with; and perhaps the concept of homage to someone might be identified.

· You Try It ·

Select a story or excerpt that your students will be reading. Choose 5–10 Tier Two words that you would like them to learn. Develop definitions for the words. Then, pair the words in a question format so that students have to consider how meanings interact in order to respond. You may want to refer to the model on page 89.

HIGH SCHOOL EXAMPLE

The example for high school is based on the opening chapter of *Wuthering Heights* by Emily Bronte (1847/1961), and it uses the text in a somewhat different way as the centerpiece for vocabulary work. It begins with a few words from the opening paragraphs of the book, because what happens so early in the novel is that the persona of Heathcliff begins to be developed. In just the first paragraph, his character begins to fall into place around the concept of *misanthrope*. More words can be introduced that have some connection to the concepts that the author is communicating about Heathcliff and the setup for the story.

For this example, we would begin by introducing the words *misanthrope*, *solitary*, *reserve*, and *inhospitable* before reading the first chapter. Here are the definitions we would use:

Target words	Definitions
misanthrope	someone who dislikes and distrusts humankind
solitary	existing alone; remote from civilization
reserve[d]	holding back in speech or manner; keeping one's feelings hidden
inhospitable	not welcoming to guests

Facets of Word Meaning

This activity is a discussion of the words introduced so far in order to consider what the similar core of them is that relates to Heathcliff. The central concept here seems to be one of "distance"—in particular, Heathcliff's personal distance from human society. We also add some further words that seem to fit the portrait of Heathcliff that the author is painting. The following outlines the basis for discussion:

- A misanthrope is defined as "someone who dislikes and distrusts humankind," yet a misanthrope is part of humankind. Can this word be used for animals?
- Would a misanthropic ape, for example, be one who hates other apes or who hates humans? (The point here is that the essence of

the word is contempt or loathing for your fellows, making yourself distant from others of your kind. That notion of distance is an important one in describing Heathcliff and his environs.)

- What other words and phrases in the text support this picture of Heathcliff keeping himself apart? (*solitary*: "removed from the stir of society")
- What kind of feeling does *solitary* give you? Does the word imply loneliness? Dislike of others' company? How is it used?
- What is the quality of Heathcliff's reserve? Here it would be important to bring up that *reserve(d)* is often associated with positive qualities, such as dignity or maturity. Or someone's seeming reserve might spring from shyness. But the essence is distance: "held or kept back" (also "cautious in one's words and actions").
- Consider introducing the words *alienate* and *estrange* into the discussion
  —*alienate*: to cause someone to become unfriendly to you or to your point of view
  —*estrange*: to put at a [psychological] distance; most often used rather formally to describe what has happened to a relationship with a spouse or other family members

Is Heathcliff's reserve meant to alienate or estrange? Help students realize that these two words relate to the concept of keeping personal distance that is emerging about Heathcliff. Prompt students to note that an important distinction is that with these words the distance is more active—holding or pushing others back emotionally, not merely keeping back oneself.

- Is *inhospitable* active or passive? (Either could probably be defended.)
- Some further words might be added here that describe the manner of someone who is inhospitable: *terse, brusque, curt*. They are very similar, although with shadings: *terse* is brief and emotionless; *brusque* carries the idea of roughness; *curt* is brief or tense, usually implying anger or at least impatience.
- Consider that a place can also be called inhospitable. What would such a place be like?
- Introduce the word *recluse*, someone who has removed himself from society. What does a recluse share with a misanthrope? What is the emotional component here?

The point of the activity is to get students to think about the words beyond their definitions, and to explore how they fit together.

Record the Words

Have students record the word meanings and some examples of their use in their word journals. The examples can merely be notes from the above discussion to help students recall the ideas that have been developed about the words.

Students' Use of Words

Have students write sentences for each word, but provide some hooks around which they can form their thoughts. Begin with a group discussion of questions such as the following, and then assign individually written sentences:

- Can you think of anyone you'd call a *misanthrope*? What does he or she do that would cause you to label him or her so?
- Do you ever feel *solitary*? What does it feel like?
- How do you respond to someone who acts *inhospitable* toward you?
- What are different ways people show *reserve*, and what different messages do they give?

Students might also be asked to write sentences for the initially introduced words (*misanthrope, solitary, reserve,* and *inhospitable*) and to include as many of the additional words as they can within those sentences.

Relationships among Words

The development of semantic relationships for older students can be done by adding more words to those under study. A good expansion to the collection of words in the example we have been considering is a set of words that is in opposition to the antisocial, distant concepts embodied in the target words. For example:

- *Philanthropist* is definitionally the opposite of *misanthrope*, but it is used very differently. Although *philanthropist* is defined as "a lover of humankind," it is used almost exclusively to designate people who give large sums of money to charity. It is unlikely to hear someone who enjoys the company of other people described as a philanthropist. From such discussion, prompt a search for a functional opposite to *misanthrope.*

- *Gregarious*, defined as "seeking and enjoying the company of others," seems in opposition to *solitary*—not alone or reserved. Discussion should note that the concept of gregarious includes not holding back but going out to others.
- In opposition to *inhospitable*, the word *solicitous* could be introduced.

Another aspect that could be developed is that there seem to be two dimensions of loving or hating humankind: One is a general loving, or kindness—a charitable nature. The other is on the order of personal friendship. *Misanthrope* seems to apply to both dimensions, but the more positive words seem to lean toward one or the other: *Philanthropist* applies to the general. *Gregarious* and *solicitous* seem more on the personal side. On the general side, we might explore the following:

- *Altruistic*: showing concern for the welfare of other people in general, rather than putting oneself first.
- *Benevolent*: being kind, helpful, and tolerant.

After this variety of words has been introduced, a good assignment would be to ask students to develop a character sketch of some character they have read about, or seen on television or in the movies. The character should fit the description of a misanthrope, a recluse, or a philanthropist. Students could consider the character's actions in terms of, say, at least three of the words that are being worked on, then write a description of how they fit or do not fit the character.

Another activity might be to write a letter to a newspaper editor on some issue from the point of view of a misanthrope or of a philanthropist; or a letter that alienates, or shows altruism, or is solicitous.

Beyond the Classroom

Challenge students to be on the alert for uses of the target words outside of class. A focus of this could be to sample various uses and try to "locate" these words in regard to their emotional components. That is, to what extent do they embody love, hatred, loneliness, or indifference to society? What is the relationship toward others that leads one to become a misanthrope or a philanthropist?—To live a solitary life or a gregarious existence? Their sighting of words can be good takeoff points for discussion as well.

Another place the collection of word sightings might lead is to have students formulate their own definitions based on the uses that have been collected. Reformulating their own definitions could help organize their growing understanding of a word and thus deepen it. Creating their own definitions based on the uses they find could also help students see the limitations of definitions that appear in dictionaries. This might help them not to rely on definitions and illustrate how much more than a definition is needed to truly get a grasp on a word's meaning.

▪ *You Try It* ▪

Have your students go on a scavenger hunt by searching magazines and newspapers to find words that interest them and that they would like to learn.

ASSESSMENT

Assessing what is learned about words relates to an issue we discussed at the outset of this book, that is, what does it mean to know a word? For example, a learner may be able to supply a synonym for a word but not know how to use it, or understand the context in which it appears but be unable to express its meaning. Such different configurations of knowledge would allow a learner to succeed on some kinds of assessments but not on others. So, when considering what kinds of assessment are appropriate, it is important to first consider the kind of learning that is the goal.

The most widely used measure of word knowledge is the multiple-choice format, such as the assessment we used earlier at the end of the "eyes" vocabulary cycle. The results of a multiple-choice test may be greatly influenced by the nature of the distracters—the incorrect choices. Distracters can introduce ideas that may confuse a learner by interfering with what the learner knows about a word. On the other hand, if the distracters are very different form the meaning of the target word, a learner can get the item correct even with very limited knowledge of the word.

The changeable nature of multiple-choice items, however, can be used to advantage, to create tests that are purposely easier or more difficult and thus tap different levels of word knowledge. Consider, for example, a test item for *diligent* whose choices are (a) fast, (b) hardworking, (c) lost, and (d) punished. Compare that to the thinking required to select the correct choice for *diligent* from among (a) making a lot of money, (b) working at an interesting job, (c) always trying one's best, and (d) remembering everything.

Some researchers have taken a pessimistic view of the usefulness of multiple-choice tests (Kameenui et al., 1987), and some are more positive about their usefulness (Curtis, 1987). Curtis argues that, despite their drawbacks, they do provide some useful information. They give reliable indications of the relative range of an individual's vocabulary and correlate rather strongly with measures of reading comprehension. As a school assessment measure, they give useful information about where a student stands in vocabulary development in relation to his or her peers.

In sorting out issues related to assessment of vocabulary knowledge, it is useful to return to the notion that word knowledge falls along a continuum and to consider where along the continuum word knowledge can be assessed by different measures. Curtis (1987) has demonstrated that different pictures of word knowledge emerge from different criteria by testing fifth graders on a set of words using several different measures. She found that on a checklist where students were asked to respond *yes* if they knew a word, students' reporting was correct about 80% of the time. When asked to explain the meaning of the words, 70% could pass a very easy criterion such as describing *invent* as "to invent a machine." When the criterion involved giving an example or partial explanation, 50% of the responses were correct. Only 20% were correct for a conservative criterion that required synonyms or complete explanations.

A very important consideration is Curtis's (1981) finding that the completeness or precision of knowledge in an individual's vocabulary repertoire differentiates high- and low-ability college students. In her study, undergraduates took a traditional multiple-choice test and then were interviewed about the tested words. From the interviews, Curtis found that low-ability students not only knew fewer of the tested words but also had less knowledge of the words they knew. Specifically, they were only able to provide correct explanations for about half the words they had gotten correct on the multiple-choice test. This finding points to the need both to teach words deeply and to measure them deeply.

There are a variety of tasks that can assess deeper levels of word knowledge. Many of the formats that we used in the activities developed for our vocabulary program can also be used as assessment formats. Consider the following:

- Ask students what words mean.
- Have students create examples such as these:
  —Describe how someone acts that shows they are *diligent*.
  —Tell about a time you were *perplexed*.
  —Describe some things that could make a person feel *miserable*.
- Present items that ask students to distinguish between an example of a word and a nonexample of a word, such as those presented as an instructional activity at the beginning of this chapter. Both the example and the nonexample should be designed to present situations that have similar features and thus require student thinking that zeros in on the meaning of the target word.

proclaim

A woman refuses to talk to reporters about the election.	A women tells reports which candidate won the election.

commend

Your teacher tells you to have your parents come in for a conference.	Your teacher tells your parents how well you are doing in school.

mention

Our neighbors once told us that they had lived in Florida.	Our neighbors are always talking about when they lived in Florida.

- Ask students to describe what is alike and/or different for pairs of words that are semantically similar (Graves, 1980). The following word pairs would be useful in such an assessment:
  —*berate/retort*
  —*seize/embrace*
  —*acquaintance/ally*
  —*exotic/unique*
  —*extraordinary/peculiar*
- Ask students to place word phrases on a word line that represents a continuum, and to explain their placement of the various items. An important point here is that there is no correct ordering of the items. The value of the format is in eliciting students explanations that involve target word meanings. Also, the fact that this format is fun is a nice dimension to add to assessment. Below are several examples:

How much energy does it take to . . .

1. *meander* down the hall?
2. *vault* over a car?
3. *banter* with your best friend for an hour?
4. *berate* someone at the top of your voice?
5. *stalk* a turtle?
6. be a *spectator* at a concert?

Least energy ——————————————————— Most energy

How happy would you be . . .

1. after *trudging* home through the rain?
2. if the President *commended* you for being brave?
3. if your mother *urged* you to have a second piece of cake?
4. if you thought someone was *stalking* you?
5. if a herd of sheep *meandered* into your living room?
6. if everyone in your class looked *glum*?

Least happy ——————————————————— Most happy

How surprised would you be if . . .

1. you saw your friend *vault* over the moon?
2. your teacher *commended* you for doing good work?

3. a dog started *bantering* with you?
4. the mayor *urged* everyone to leave town?
5. a coach *berated* his football team for not making a touchdown?
6. a rabbit *trudged* through a garden?

Least surpised ——————————————————— Most surprised

Earlier in this chapter we described a "context interpretation" task in which students responded to questions about sentences containing target words. The important point about this task is that it requires students to go beyond thinking about a word's definition. Rather, it requires applying the word's meaning to understand the context of its use. The task can be made more or less challenging depending on whether the contexts show typical or not so typical uses for the target word. Note that in the examples below, the first item is more challenging, as someone is commended in an unexpected situation—for destroying something in anger; the other examples show more typical uses:

- When father heard that Lisa had ripped up the letter from Steve, father *commended* her for it. What do you think father thought of Steve?
- When Sam and I arrived at Alvin's front door, I had to *urge* Sam to knock on the door. How do you think Sam felt about going to Alvin's house?
- Rhonda sent out wedding invitations to all the family, including Uncle Charles, who was a *hermit*. What do you think Uncle Charles's answer was to the invitation?
- Mr. Robinson, the high school principal, was in a very good mood after his meeting with the *philanthropist*. Why do you think Mr. Robinson was happy?
- Mary thought that Jim was *ridiculing* her when he said that the cake she made looked beautiful. How do you think Mary thought her cake looked?
- Jerome told us he was a *novice*, but when we heard him play the piano we knew he had been kidding us. What do you think Jerome's piano playing sounded like?
- Everyone whom Paul met at his new school was very much alike,

except for Dan who was an *extrovert*. How do you think Dan acted toward Paul?

- At the baseball game Tony thought his chances of hitting a home run were *thwarted* when Rusty came on to pitch. What do you think Tony thought of Rusty's pitching?

The message about vocabulary assessment is that the assessments should match the goals. If fairly straightforward knowledge is the goal, then multiple-choice items can be appropriate. If deeper knowledge is the goal, then the more complex formats noted above are more likely to provide the kind of information that will allow teachers to determine whether students have gained complete, precise, or deep understanding.

▪ *You Try It* ▪

Select one or more of the assessments:

- Write some sentence stems for words that your students are learning.
- Create some questions that have students choosing one of two vocabulary words as the answer.
- Develop some assessment items for words that you have selected for your students to learn.

IN SUMMARY

Throughout this chapter, and indeed throughout this book, we have emphasized the importance of keeping vocabulary work going—following up the introduction of meanings—and using words outside of class. The reasons that these are so essential to learning new words is that words can only truly be learned through use. The nuances, subtleties, and characteristics of a word's role in the language can only be understood through repeated exposures to the word in a variety of contexts. A definition, no matter how well crafted, can never communicate all of this. That is why students need to look for contexts of use and bring those into the classroom for discussion, so that each context can add dimension to what is known about a word. The need for multiple uses becomes even more critical at the upper grades because the words are more sophisticated and thus more multidimensional and distinctions among them more subtle.

• *Your Turn* •

We invite you to use what you have learned in this chapter to develop some ideas for supporting students in thinking about a set of words that you have selected from a text that they are reading.

Describe your rationale for selecting the words. Then, develop questions to help students explore the facets of each word's meaning. Finally, create some assignments that will engage students in using the words in meaningful ways.

CHAPTER 6

Making the Most
of Natural Contexts

A number of years ago, Mark, one of our children who was about 9 at the time, was reading a Hardy Boys book. As his mother passed his room, he called out, "What does *rendezvous* [mispronouncing the French word as ren/des/vus] mean?" His mother, not understanding the word the way he said it, went into his room and said, "Let me see how it's used." Mark showed her the sentence: "The boys would rendezvous at the cave." Like a good teacher, his mother pronounced the word correctly (rahn-day-voo) and suggested that Mark look at the words around it and figure out what he thought it meant. Mark replied, "To eat." After quizzing him a little further, Mark's mother learned he had reached that conclusion because the boys had been planning a picnic and deciding what kind of food each was going to bring.

In this scenario, what the mother-teacher was drawing on was suggestions from methods classes and from the teacher's editions that accompany student texts for reading and language arts. Indeed, the scope and sequence of skills and strategies almost always includes a reference to context clues. In fact, using context clues is usually listed as one of the main strategies for figuring out the meaning of words, coming right in between "ask someone" and "look it up in the dictionary." The suggestions for teaching students how to use context clues emphasizes the need for students to pay attention to the words around an unfamiliar word, searching for clues that will unlock the meaning of the unknown word.

Usually teachers are left with little more than that general directive, or a suggestion to point out some particularly helpful contexts, such as those that include a synonym or point of contrast. The purpose of this chapter is to provide teachers with some specific strategies for helping students make the most of the natural contexts in which they encounter unfamiliar words.

A CONTEXT FOR THIS CHAPTER

Our readers may be surprised that we have written a chapter about teaching students to derive word meanings from natural contexts, given our strong assertions about the difficulty of doing so. Emphatically, we do not retract the concerns we have discussed. Rather, we keep the concerns alive in our discussion of what might be done to help students gain word meaning information from natural contexts.

To set the scene for the kind of instructional recommendations we will make in this chapter, let us provide a brief sketch of the road we traveled that led us to our current perspective. In our earliest forays into vocabulary instruction, we noticed that there was a kind of mantra about how to provide vocabulary instruction: "Have students use context clues." For decades, the theme of context clues seemed to dominate vocabulary instruction. The strongest variant of the theme involved working with categories of context clues that investigators seemed to believe were highly predictive of word meaning. The focus of work on vocabulary through the 1940s, '50s, and '60s seemed to be on identifying and refining these categories of context clues and promoting the teaching of them to students (e.g., Ames, 1966/1967; Artley, 1943; McCullough 1943, 1958; Rankin & Overholser, 1969). Some examples of clue types from the various classification schemes are presented below:

contrast	Unlike Sarah who was graceful and elegant, Milly was quite *clumsy*.
linked synonyms or appositives	The strongest of the group, all people of height, athletic ability, and *stamina*, were dispatched to protect the camp.

The results of studies directed at the use of the categories were usually at least somewhat successful in teaching students about the clue types. However, it doesn't take long to recognize that teaching such clues through contrived contexts, which is the only way one could do it, is unlikely to transfer to natural contexts.

Our next major foray into the universe of context was an examination of the recommendations that several basal reading programs made for helping students derive meaning from context. We found two pervasive recommendations: (1) Teach specific types of context clues such as the kinds noted above. (2) Have students derive meaning in the course of reading. Having already rejected the first, we explored the second direction by engaging in the study (discussed in Chapter 1) in which we categorized the types of information available in natural contexts (i.e., misdirective, nondirective, generally directive, directive) and demonstrated that even adults could only reliably gain information from the most directive contexts.

Our next turn on the vocabulary context road was to explore *how* students of high and low verbal ability actually use context (McKeown, 1985). The exploration focused on the process of deriving word meaning from context, in which a learner first recognizes a word as unknown, then selects information in the context that constrains the word meaning, next combines relevant clues into a hypothesis for the word's meaning, and finally refines that hypothesis upon encountering further information. A study was designed to examine that process by looking at the reasoning learners engaged in as they worked through series of contexts with increasing information for identifying target words (McKeown, 1985).

The results of our study pointed to differences in the reasoning processes used by high- and low-ability students as they tried to figure out word meanings. The differences emerged as three characteristics that less-skilled students engage in more than high-ability students did while attempting to derive word meaning through context.

One was a **limited use of context**, in that students focused too narrowly on the context and failed to consider key aspects that were needed to derive the meaning of a target word. As an illustration, consider the case of the pseudoword *laked* as a stand-in for *dragged: The carpenter laked several heavy pieces of lumber to the middle of his workroom and* *carefully placed them against an old table.* Deciding that *laked* meant "burned" because "You can burn wood" is an example of one student's limited use of the context. The only consideration from the given context is that wood can burn. But it doesn't make sense that the carpenter would burn wood that he had "carefully placed."

The second characteristic is **attributing the meaning of the entire context to the target word**. Classic examples of this date back to Werner and Kaplan's (1952) landmark study. They provide the example that the meaning of *bordicks* in the sentence "People talk about the bordicks of others, but don't talk about their own" was described by a young student as "People talk about other people and don't like to talk about themselves" (p. 15).

The third problematic characteristic is going beyond the limits of the meaning of the context and developing a **scenario** into which a meaning might fit. What happens in such cases is that the student selects a possible meaning for a word and then creates a rationale to accommodate that meaning. The result is a bogus relationship between the student's suggested word meaning and the context. For example, in the case of the context sentence, "Because I like corn I would like to *steen* some," a student responded, "It could be 'sell' because if you make some money, you could grow some corn and sell it."

The recommendation from McKeown's (1985) study was that instructional strategies needed to focus on the *process* of deriving word meanings, in contrast to the *product* of coming up with the right meaning of an unknown word.

THE PROCESS OF USING CONTEXT

Providing support to students for deriving word meanings became the focus of an instructional study undertaken by Goerss, Beck, and McKeown (1999). The study sought to address the problems students had in using context by developing instruction that started with teacher modeling of how one might consider what an unfamiliar word in context might mean and lots of opportunities for students to engage in interactive practice. To explore whether the instruction was effective, Goerss and colleagues took low-skilled readers through seven instructional sessions in which they were given a variety of natural contexts and supported in deriving word meaning information through the specific instructional procedures (which will be specified in detail later) developed for the study. Over the course of the study, students showed strong improvements in being able to identify relevant information from contexts and using that information to develop reasonable hypotheses about a word's meaning.

To provide a sense of the kinds of improvements that students made over the course of the study, we present a portion of a transcript of one student's interactions with context during the first training session, as well as a transcript from a later session. The student is Lisa, a 13-year-old sixth grader who had been in remedial reading programs since second grade. Prior to engagement in the study, she exhibited all of the problems described earlier in using context to derive meanings. One problem was her inability to separate a specific meaning for an unfamiliar word from the rest of the context. Below, Lisa's response to a context with *huddling* provides an example of this problem:

> *Even knowing help would come shortly didn't make it pleasant. Cobie sat down <u>huddling</u> her arms and face against her knees for warmth.*

The investigator led Lisa through the first several steps of the instructional procedure, and Lisa recognized that in the sentence Cobie was trying to get warm. However, when Lisa was asked what *huddling* might mean, her responses attributed the meaning of the entire sentence to that word. (Note: "Inv" in the transcript stands for the investigator who conducted the interview.)

LISA: She could be trying to get warm.

The investigator attempted to describe *huddling* in order to help Lisa find a specific meaning, but Lisa was unresponsive. Finally, the investigator demonstrated *huddling* with her arms and face against her knees.

INV: If someone was doing this, what would you call it?
LISA: She was cold.

This example is in sharp contrast to Lisa's approach to using context in the final (seventh) session. Here, she was able to distinguish the meaning of the word from the context and think of possible meanings for it. Consider the following context and how Lisa approaches uncovering what *conscientious* might mean:

> She wouldn't have forgotten. Sister Frances isn't like that. She's very *conscientious*; in fact, she says so herself and expects all of us to be too.

In the transcript below, Lisa begins to think through the context, describing several aspects she has identified as holding clues to the meaning of *conscientious*:

> What is happening is Sister Frances is talking or telling. Some clues might be *forgotten*, *Sister Frances*, and *expects all of us to be*.

Lisa then goes on to explore what these clues might yield as a meaning for *conscientious*. Note that she is able to discern the most meaningful aspect of the context—that *conscientiousness* is a quality that Sister Frances has and expects others to have—and keep her focus on it as she generated possible meanings. Lisa said:

> *Conscientious* could be "nice" because she said so herself and ex-pects everyone to be like that. Or "caring" because it is how she wants everyone else to be. *Friendly*, because she is telling every-body that she is like that and she wants everybody to be like, that's how she . . . the way she told people to act.

Lisa does not come up with the meaning of *conscientious*, but in the context provided there are not sufficient clues to enable her to do so. What she was able to do is provide some reasonable possibilities, and all the possibilities were in the right domain: *Conscientious* is a positive quality. So, had she been independently reading the text, she would at least not have misunderstood the general notion. Moreover, having put *conscientious* into a positive domain, the next time Lisa comes across a context with the word, she may be able to build on what she has figured out and get closer to an understanding of the word.

Meet with a few students one on one and ask them to read a passage that you have selected. The passage should include some words that are unfamiliar to students. Ask students to talk about what they think the word means and what information in the passage supports their ideas.

THE INSTRUCTIONAL SEQUENCE

The instruction we designed for our context research took students through the process of deriving word meaning and allowed them to see that different contexts offered different levels of information about word meaning. The instructional model started with an investigator modeling the process and then scaffolding it as responsibility was gradually released to the student. The instructional sequence included five components that started with (1) the text being read and paraphrased, they required the student to (2) explain what the text was about and (3) provide an initial notion of the word's meaning; the sequence also required the student to (4) consider whether the context would allow other potential meanings; and finally (5) the information that had been established through the dialogue was summarized. The enactment of the instructional sequence is represented in examples from several transcripts in which Goerss and colleagues (1999) interacted with students.

The purpose of the initial step, **read/paraphrase**, was to introduce the context and paraphrase it in a way that put emphasis on the unfamiliar word. Either the investigator or the student could do the reading and paraphrasing. In the example below, the investigator does both:

"As for Rusty, he scowled at Mary before stamping out of the room. 'And I'm not coming back either, see!' " Now, let's kind of reread these sentences to figure out what's happening. Rusty does this *scowled* thing at Mary and then stamps out of the room. As he does this he says, "And I'm not coming back either, see!"

As noted in the foregoing example, the investigator does the paraphrasing, but it is essential that as students get acquainted with the approach they are given the responsibility to figure out what is being said.

The second step in the instructional sequence was to **establish meaning of the context**. This is done in order to get students to fully consider the meaning of the context and prevent them from an isolated focus on the word. To help accomplish this, after the initial reading of an item, a teacher can encourage students to consider the information by asking, "What's being said?" or "What's going on?" or "Tell us what those sentences are all about." This in itself can go a long way toward helping students become sensitive to the relationship between a context and an unfamiliar word. Below, note that the student is successful in establishing the meaning of the context:

INV:	What's happening in these sentences?
STUDENT:	Rusty is mad at Mary about something, and he stamped out of the room.
INV:	Good, is there anything else?
STUDENT:	Well, he yelled at her as he went out the door that he wasn't coming back.

Note that when the investigator asked, "Is there anything else?" she was looking for the student to examine the context further so that the student might generate some more information—beyond Rusty being mad—that might be helpful in generating possible meanings for the unfamiliar word.

In the third step, **initial identification/rationale**, the student was asked to provide some sense of what the word might be and a rationale for how the context supported that choice. Note that, in the example of this step below, the student is able to generate a plausible meaning, "yelled," with a rationale that includes helpful context:

INV:	What do you think *scowled* might mean?
STUDENT:	"Yelled."
INV:	Why do you think it is "yelled"?
STUDENT:	Well, he is mad at her and then he yelled that he wasn't coming back.

If a student did not have a response at this point or failed to use context information, the investigator guided the student by reviewing the **establish context meaning** step, perhaps drawing attention to relevant context clues. Then, the student was encouraged to provide an idea of the meaning of a target word, not necessarily an exact word. In the dialogue below, which was quite typical, note that the investigator returns to the context and specifically asks the student to generate possible meanings:

INV: What do you think *scowled* means?

STUDENT: (*No response.*)

INV: Let's look at the sentence with *scowled* again: "As for Rusty, he scowled at Mary before stamping out of the room." When someone stamps out of a room, what do you think they are feeling?

STUDENT: Mad or upset.

INV: Right, so if Rusty is mad or upset, what are some things he might do at Mary?

STUDENT: Yell or throw something.

The fourth step, **consider further possibilities**, is to help students examine more possibilities and refrain from the expectation that it is necessary or even possible to find one right meaning for every unfamiliar word. This step might proceed something like the dialogue presented here:

INV: Can you think of some other possible meanings?

STUDENT: Make faces at her.

INV: Why do you say "make faces at her"?

STUDENT: If you are mad at someone, you might make a face at her before you stamp out of the room.

INV: Can you think of anything else *scowled* might mean?

STUDENT: Shake your fist.

INV: What made you say that?

STUDENT: I shake my fist when I'm mad at my sister.

Note that the student was able to generate two other possible meanings using the context and experience.

In the fifth and last step, **summarize**, the information that had been generated in the dialogue about the unfamiliar word was pulled together. The intent here was to bring together information so that it would be available to the student to reconsider and then draw conclusions about what was known about the word's meaning. As an example, consider the following:

INV: What do we know about *scowled*?

STUDENT: It is something Rusty did at Mary.

INV: And . . . ?

STUDENT: He was mad because he stamped out of the room telling her he wasn't coming back. It could be "yelled" or "shook his fist" or "made an angry face at her."

INV: Any one of those might be possible meanings for *scowled* based on these sentences. *Scowled does* mean one that you suggested—"made an angry face."

The whole point of the five steps is to get the students to really think through what is being talked about and notice what information in the text might relate to a target word. From there, it becomes a trial-and-error process to see if a word that comes to mind fits the whole context and, if not, to generate alternatives. An important point, however, is that the learner needs to be fully cognizant of the varying amounts of information that are available from contexts, and needs to know when to stop the process—as it might not be possible to come up with a likely meaning of a word.

WORKING WITH A GROUP OF STUDENTS

The instructional sequence explained above can be used in a range of informal to formal situations, with one or several students or with the whole class. And, depending on the situation, all the steps or just one or two steps can be used. The examples from the Goerss et al. (1999) study showed the use of all the steps and involved working with an individual student. But it has been our experience that trying to figure out the meaning of a word from context is enriched when a group of students, including the whole class, is involved. We provide some examples of the procedures used in whole-class situations.

In a section from *Charlotte's Web* by E. B. White (1952) in which Wilbur, the pig, asks, Templeton, the rat, "Will you play with me?" Templeton responds that he doesn't "know the meaning of the word." So, Wilbur describes some of the things one does when playing, to which Templeton says: "I never do those things if I can avoid them." At this point the teacher decides to pursue the meaning of *avoid* and the following dialogue occurs:

> TEACHER: What's Templeton saying here?
>
> STUDENT: He doesn't like to do those things.
>
> TEACHER: What do you think *avoid* means?
>
> STUDENT: "Never do those things."
>
> TEACHER: So, *avoid* means "not to do something"?
>
> STUDENTS: (*Several students seem to agree.*)
>
> TEACHER: *Avoid* does mean" "to stay away from something."

In this case, identifying the meaning of *avoid* worked well. It worked well because the text information was adequate for inferring the meaning, but we also submit that it worked well because the teacher started with establishing the message of the text segment before going directly to questioning about what *avoid* might mean.

Below, we provide examples of a situation where deriving a meaning is much more difficult. The example comes from the scene in which Templeton leaves Wilbur and goes into a tunnel that he has dug. Then, the text says:

> *Templeton was a crafty rat and he had things pretty much his own way. The tunnel was an example of his skill and cunning. The tunnel enabled him to get from the barn to his hiding place under the pig trough without coming out into the open.*

The following exchange captures how the teacher pursues the meaning of *cunning*:

TEACHER: What's happening here?

STUDENT: Templeton goes in his tunnel.

TEACHER: What do we know about the tunnel?

STUDENT: He made it.

STUDENT: Nobody sees him.

TEACHER: What's it mean, "The tunnel was an example of his skill and cunning"?

STUDENT: He was good at making the tunnel.

TEACHER: Okay, he was good at it, so that's an example of his skill, but what do you think *cunning* means?

STUDENT: His digging skill . . .

TEACHER: Well, he did dig the tunnel, but *cunning* is telling us something more about Templeton. Remember when [name of the third student who spoke] told us that he goes into the tunnel so nobody sees him. So, what's that say about Templeton?

STUDENT: He dug a deep tunnel so nobody could see him.

STUDENT: He's smart.

STUDENT: He's sneaky.

TEACHER: Great! Templeton is smart and sneaky! And that's what *cunning* means. *Cunning* means "to be clever and sneaky."

The *cunning* example is an instance of going through the process using a context that has several clues to the word's meaning, as well as information that could distract and lead to other possible meanings.

The next situation involves a text that does not have enough information to provide a direction for a target word's meaning. It occurs in the text after Templeton declines to play with Wilbur and explains that the way he wants to spend his time is

eating, gnawing, spying and hiding. I am a glutton but not a merry-maker. Right now I'm on my way to your trough to eat your breakfast, since you haven't got sense enough to eat it yourself.

TEACHER: What does this tell us about Templeton?

STUDENT: He doesn't want to play.

STUDENT: He's going to eat Wilbur's breakfast?

STUDENT: He thinks Wilbur is dumb because he didn't eat his breakfast.

TEACHER: Okay, it also says that Templeton likes "eating, gnawing, spying and hiding. I am a glutton but not a merry-maker."

TEACHER: What do you think a glutton is?

STUDENT: Somebody who doesn't like to have fun.

STUDENT: Like somebody who spies and steals things.

TEACHER: Those ideas show good thinking because those are ideas that are coming through about Templeton. But *glutton* means "somebody who likes to eat a lot and is very greedy for food." You know, there really was no way for you to figure that out for sure because there was lots of other information about Templeton and it was hard to tell just what that information was telling you about him being a glutton.

The teacher then went on to make the point to the students that sometimes when they are reading they will not be able to figure out the meaning of a word they don't know. But she complimented them on the good thinking that they had done about *glutton* and said that such thinking would often help them get ideas about what words mean.

IN SUMMARY

If teachers wants to hone their skills to support students' abilities to derive the meanings of words from natural contexts, the following advice may help:

- Anticipate that at first students will tend to engage in inappropriate meaning-deriving characteristics: limited use of context, attributing the meaning of a word to the meaning of the entire context, and creating a scenario for a word's possible meaning.
- Keep in mind that natural contexts do not act in logical and sys-

tematic ways and vary widely in the amount of information they provide about a given word.

- Because of the unreliability of natural contexts, instruction needs to be presented as a *process* of figuring out meaning within an individual contexts, rather than focusing on the *product*—a word's meaning.
- When implementing instruction, always start with asking students to explain what is going on in the portion of text being read, and then what the word might mean.

▪ *Your Turn* ▪

Select some passages from a text that your students are reading, and identify some words in contexts that they can use to figure out the meanings of the words. Prepare for your work with students by noting the questions you will ask for each step in the instructional sequence explained above:

1. Read/paraphrase the text being read.
2. Establish meaning of the context.
3. Provide an initial identification/rationale.
4. Consider further possibilities.
5. Summarize.

[CHAPTER 7]

Enriching
the Verbal Environment

Ms. K's fourth-grade classroom:

Ms. K:	Good afternoon.
Darleen:	Salutations, Ms. K!
Melissa:	Greetings!
Daniel:	Hello!
Ms. K:	So, how was recess?
Beth:	Invigorating.
Thomas:	Exhausting. We played football!
Laura:	Delightful. There was a lovely breeze.
Robert:	Abbreviated. It was too short for me!

The above exchange is an example of the kind of conversation that might take place in a classroom that provides a rich verbal environment for students, an environment in which words are valued as interesting and important. In such an environment, literature and poetry that celebrate language are shared. For example, it is likely that the teacher and students in the above exchange have been reading *The Phantom Tollbooth* by Norton Juster (1964), a fantasy in which a Word Market is only one of the stopping places that Milo, the main character, visits on his journey through Dictionopolis.

To this point, we have mostly considered texts as sources of words, but there are many other sources. The purpose of this chapter is to consider those other sources and to show how they can be used to bring words to life in the classroom. One major source is the teacher's own language as illustrated below:

DARLEEN: Ms. K, look at Melissa's backpack!

Ms. K: (*admiring the stickers and sparkly appliqués*) Oh, Melissa, I really like the way you've *embellished* your backpack!

DARLEEN: Embellished? What's that mean?

MELISSA: It means my backpack's cool!

The above exchange is an example of a teacher being alert to opportunities to apply sophisticated words to everyday situations. A teacher's language and imagination brought to bear on situations and happenings in the classroom are a major source for creating a rich verbal environment. Ms. H, the first-grade teacher we discussed in Chapter 4, spontaneously but judiciously labeled situations with "grown-up" words. Here are some favorites from her classroom:

- A student who worked and worked at writing his name more clearly was called *persistent*.
- When children talked about others "copying them," she offered *imitate*.
- When the children completed good work, she called it *exceptional*.
- When she announced that an individual who had a particular skill would be visiting, he was called an *expert*.
- When the class was behaving well, she called them *mature*.
- When the brother of one of their favorite teachers was killed, she said that the teacher was feeling very *forlorn*.

Ms. H then placed such words on a bulletin board with the label "Wonderful Words." When possible she would use them in her conversations with the children.

WHAT IS A RICH VERBAL ENVIRONMENT?

The idea of a rich verbal environment is to have words in play nearly all of the time; perhaps we can think of it as a classroom rife with words. This means both a frequent use of words that have been taught and taking any and all opportunities to add words to students' surroundings. Even if a teacher can't keep track of all of them, it is valuable to sprinkle the environment generously with words!

The idea of sprinkling the environment with words may seem in contrast to what we have stressed in earlier chapters, the need for multiple encounters with words for them to truly become known. But here we are talking about an *additional* goal of vocabulary instruction—that of having students become generally alert to words and word use, to become interested in words. It is true that not all of the words that appear in the students' environment will be learned. But, then again, if students do not encounter new words, there is no possibility of learning them. Exposure will provide students with a chance to pick up and use some words, or an opportunity to recognize other words that they will eventually meet in subsequent experiences.

PAYING ATTENTION TO WORDS

A good starting point for creating a rich verbal environment is to establish the importance of paying attention to words. One way to emphasize such importance is to encourage students to notice examples of words they are learning in school being used in contexts outside of school. As we described in Chapter 5, extension of word use beyond the classroom was one of the important aspects of our vocabulary research. We found that gimmicks can increase the chances that this will occur. The gimmick we used in our vocabulary studies was the Word Wizard chart. This was a chart of students' names with space to add tally marks as they brought in sightings or uses of words that had been introduced to their class. They could earn points for reporting sightings of target words or for using them.

Before introducing the Word Wizard notion to our fourth-grade vocabulary research classrooms, we engaged in an "advertising campaign" about the opportunity to become a Word Wizard. Specifically, we distributed leaflets entitled "You Can Be a Word Wizard!" The leaflet described with engaging graphics the different categories that students could achieve, with the highest being, of course, Word Wizard. Other categories included Word Wildcat, Word Whirlwind, Word Winner, Word Worker, and Word Watcher. On another fold of the leaflet were descriptions of how points could be earned. For example:

> If you hear a word—on TV, on the radio, on the street, or at home— you can earn 1 point. Just tell your teacher where you heard or saw the word and how it was used.

On the back fold of the leaflet students were told to—

- Look for your name on the Word Wizard chart.
- Watch for special events for Word Wizard points.

Points were tallied every few weeks, and students received certificates based on their totals. The certificates were designed around the different categories.

To earn their points, students had to describe the contexts in which the words were used. An interesting feature of this activity that we discovered is that students' fabrications still accomplished the purposes of the activity. That is, sometimes students made up a story about using or hearing the word even though it did not occur. A long remembered example was the boy who reported to the teacher, "I told my mother I was so *famished*, I was going to *devour* everything in the refrigerator, and that I didn't care whether it was *nutritious*." Three points! One could well question the veracity of the reported incident; what cannot be questioned, however, is that the student had used the words in a context beyond the classroom.

We can guarantee from our experience that this activity is successful! The fourth graders in the participating classes went absolutely wild with bringing in words. So much so that a constant topic of conversation at our meetings with the teachers was how to manage the enormity of tallying the students' points!

Since using the Word Wizard in our studies and describing it to teachers, we have seen teachers develop a host of variations that are useful for similar purposes and across various grade levels. In Ms. H's classroom, the Word Wizard device she created allowed first-grade children to "show off" their new vocabulary expertise. At any time that a child could explain the meaning of three of the words under the display, she or he received each of those words on cards, as well as a Word Wizard hat. Then, with the Word Wizard hat and the three cards, the child could go through the school and any adult could read the word on one of the cards and ask the child to explain its meaning. The other teachers, and in particular the principal, got into it, and there were many oohhs and aahhs heard when a Word Wizard was in the hall!

For older students, finding words and uses for words outside of class can be part of their grade or extra credit. A posted roster with tally marks for the number of sightings can help the students know where they stand.

The discovery of examples of target words in various environments can be left up to the students' motivation, as in the case of doing so for extra credit and, indeed, for Word Wizard points. However, looking for examples of words in various environments can be primed somewhat. For example, the teacher can assign a word or several words for students to find or to invent an example or application for. The teacher might ask students to find the words *reasonable, inexpensive,* or *competitive* in newspaper or TV advertisements.

Another variation of assigning students to engage with words outside of school is to ask them to identify or create a situation that could be described by a target word. For instance, ask students to find something *whimsical* in the news, or challenge them to find as many possible applications of a short list of target words (e.g., *ultimate, diverse, unique*) as they can in one evening—using sources such as the newspaper, books they read, TV programs, or their family's conversation. This could be an individual or team competition.

Another activity for taking student's word learning beyond the classroom, which would also promote general word awareness, is to create a Suggestion Box into which students place candidate words for expanding the word pool. We discovered this notion when students involved in the vocabulary research discussed earlier spontaneously began to suggest other words that we should include in our vocabulary program. The three words we remember are *crevice, unique,* and *triumphantly.* What this indicated to us was that students were becoming increasingly aware of words in their environment, especially taking notice of words they were not familiar with.

▪ *You Try It* ▪

Create a Suggestion Box in your classroom. Challenge students to find interesting words that they would like to add to their vocabulary and place them into the Suggestion Box. Several times a week you might set aside a few minutes to pull a few words from the Suggestion Box and talk about them.

USING MATURE LANGUAGE

Beyond innovative ways to keep students' attention to target vocabulary alive, an enormously important orientation is that the classroom verbal environment be one that makes mature language a visible part of everyday practice. Teachers, through their own choice of words, should strive to have students become accustomed to hearing words they do not know, words that are beyond their current knowledge. This helps students stretch their expectations about language. It is important for students to have a glimpse of the language that is still there for them to learn and to come to believe that it is within their reach. Having unfamiliar words in the environment also encourages students to ask what words mean, which is an excellent habit to encourage. Not every use of a new word has to be in a clear, pedagogical context. Sophisticated words should be a natural part of the classroom conversation, as in the following examples:

- Use *relentless* to label a student who keeps asking, "When are you going to give us our tests back?"
- Call a student *pragmatic* if she plans ahead for completing her homework for the week.
- Comment that the weather forecast is *discouraging* if rain is predicted on a field trip day.

An important aspect of developing the verbal environment is that teachers themselves ought to become very sensitive to words. Teachers should strive to bring forth their own curiosity about words, taking time to share with students their "favorite" words. For example, one teacher told her students that she was simply fascinated by etymologies. Her students were intrigued enough to find out what she was talking about. Sharing with students their own misunderstandings of certain words is another way teachers can prompt thinking about word meanings and their uses.

To develop resources for enhancing the verbal environment teachers need to be alert to words and their uses in and out of school. For example, are there words that are used by visiting speakers at school assemblies that can be brought into the classroom?

- *secure, safeguard* from a police officer
- *preservation, refuge, regenerate* from an environmentalist
- *prominent, distinctive, illustrious* from the introduction of local celebrities

What words can be used to describe the school or the classroom?

- *spacious* hallways
- *inadequate* locker space
- *vivid* colors for the newly painted library walls

What words can be used to characterize people and places in the school?

- a *stern* assistant principal
- a music teacher with a *melodious* voice
- a gym teacher who expects *vigorous* exercise
- a *boisterous* lunchroom
- an *astonishing* talent show

Current events, both in the community and across the region and country, are other sources of interesting words. Teachers can bring urbane and sophisticated words into discussions of such events or point out word use by reporters and columnists. Storms that cause *havoc*, peace efforts that overcome seemingly *insurmountable* obstacles, court decisions based on *precedents*, *suspenseful* moments in a movie—all are grist for a our busy mill.

WORD RESOURCES

Part of a rich verbal environment are resources that students can use to discover and follow up on interesting words. Various dictionaries provide such a resource. Because dictionaries differ in their styles of defining terms, however, being able to compare across styles can be an eye-opening experience. First, checking more than one dictionary can make for a better start in zeroing in on a word's meaning. Second, seeing the variation in dictionaries can help students understand the openness and flexibility of language—particularly that there is nothing absolute about a dictionary definition.

Of special interest here are "learner's dictionaries." These resources were developed specifically for students learning English as a second language, but they are very well suited to any student of the language. They present definitions in much more accessible language than traditional dictionaries, even dictionaries created for students. A notable one is the *Collins COBUILD English Language Dictionary* (1987). This dictionary provides discursive explanations rather than traditional definitions. For example, the meaning of *sparse* is presented as follows: "Something that is sparse is small in number or amount and spread out over an area."

Unabridged dictionaries are excellent resources in classrooms for older students. It is often a memorable learning experience to look up a word such as *call* and read all of its rich and varied meanings, which number more than 60!

A thesaurus should also be available for students to consult. Encourage students to use one, but also frame discussions around what they find. Steer students away from the practice of merely substituting a word with any word they find listed with it in a thesaurus. Explore with students the similarities and differences—both great and subtle—between words that the thesaurus lists as being related. For example, consider the distinctions between the words in these pairs: *grateful* and *obliged*; *oblivious* and *forgetful*; *galvanize* and *provoke*.

Other resources that focus on words such as the games Scrabble and Password or crossword puzzles can be made available for rainy day recesses or in centers for independent learning or exploration time. Posters in the computer area of the classroom can alert students to Web sites such as those listed below, which provide fascinating word information:

Dictionary.com/Word of the Day
Factmonster.com/WordWise

If resources related to words are available and if students are given opportunities to use them, then chances are that words will become more of a focus of interest, which is exactly the situation that we hope to create.

Literature and Poetry

Reference books are not the only kinds of books to be found in a rich verbal environment. There are numerous wonderful books for students of all ages that celebrate language in fascinating, enthralling, and captivating ways. Teachers can read these books aloud to students or make them available in the classroom library. Some examples of books that draw students' attention to words are presented in Appendix B.

Stories and poems such as those described in Appendix B offer delightful contexts for discussions about words as well as word-related activities. For example, after reading about invented words, students can invent their own, complete with definitions and examples. What makes a useful definition can be discussed. After reading books about multiple-meaning words, students can create their own jokes and riddles making use of word play.

Stories and poems can also be a rich source for collecting words. For example, while reading *Catherine, Called Birdy*, historical fiction set in the Middle Ages by Karen Cushman (1994), students can suggest words to put on a bulletin board or poster with pictures or explanations. From the first chapter, students might suggest *abbey, monk, vespers, crusades, solar, privy, shire, minstrel,* and *knight.* After the words have been posted, they can be sorted into categories, such as church words, rooms and places, and people. The display can be referred to as the novel is read, and more words can be added.

Some teachers take time to share or have their students share a poem. Poems are superb sources of interesting and precise words and word combinations. The poem "Fireflies" from the collection *Joyful Noise: Poems for Two Voices* by Paul Fleischman (1988), for example, speaks of "insect calligraphers" whose vanishing messages are "fleeting graffiti." Such mellifluous phrases demonstrate how language can surprise and delight.

But What Do You *Do* with the Words?

Once words have been identified and discussed, what else is there to do? How do you treat words after they have entered the environment? The choices include how explicitly to work with the meaning and whether to keep track of words after they are introduced. Since the focus here is about creating a verbal environment with an abundant variety of words, it is not necessary to explicitly introduce the meaning of every word that you "seed" into that environment. The answer here is to focus on just a few words at a time that are kind of "kept around." Something like Ms. H's "Wonderful Words" bulletin board or simply a word list on the board is sufficient. These selected words can then be included in other vocabulary activities or Word Wizard-type challenges. And the teacher can look for multiple opportunities to sprinkle them in.

The words that are to become part of the classroom scene for a while can be selected spontaneously. Whether words will stay in the environment or only "visit" temporarily is not something that needs to be planned ahead of time. For example, the teacher may use a word that comes to mind as fitting. For instance, the students may be talking about how *lucky* a character was that he discovered a way out of a jam. The discovery came as a coincidental event, so the teacher might suggest that the situation was *fortuitous*. Then, suppose later in the day a student bales another out of a jam by lending him his extra pencil. The teacher could comment that it was quite fortuitous that a student happened to have an extra pencil that day. The two incidents with *fortuitous* might be a trigger to mark that word as one that is going to be returned to in the classroom.

What about developing the meanings of words that the teacher spontaneously uses? It is difficult to come up with a good, clear, appropriate definition. To develop an explanation of a word's meaning, start with a use of the word and they form the explanation around the context in which the word is used. It can help to compare situations in which you would and would not use it, and give further examples. For instance, a definition for the word *receptive* is probably not on the tip of a typical language user's tongue. However, getting across its meaning can be done fairly easily by forming an explanation around a context in which it occurs, such as the following one:

> "Henry was receptive to the idea of staying with his grandmother." That means that he was open to thinking about staying with his grandmother; he thought it would probably be okay. If you're receptive to something, it means you'll listen to the idea and think about it. I might be receptive to canceling homework for today if everyone gets their work done!

Another way to establish a new word's meaning is to rely on students to *eventually* figure it out. After some new word has been used, put the word on the board and ask if students know it. If not, encourage them to work toward developing a definition, based on what they can figure out about the word from the context in which it was used. Leave the word, any associations students have or clues to its meaning, and the context on the board and see what develops. If students find the word in other contexts, add those, and add to what they know about the word. Or some student might look up the word in the dictionary and the definition can be discussed.

In short, the answer to what to do with words as they enter the verbal environment is to monitor student reactions toward deciding how many words are too many, which words should be kept in play, and which should have meanings explicitly introduced.

EXPLORING WITHIN AND ACROSS WORDS

The teacher can be alert to applying words that have already been introduced, say, for an upcoming story. For example, if *irritate* had been introduced, when a noise disturbs the class, comment on the *irritation*.

Bringing attention to familiar words can also enrich the environment. There are many words that are in students' environment and that they have some passing familiarity with but may not really know much about. This is common, especially if the word is encountered only in stereotypical contexts. Students may understand that context but not really know the word. For example, what is the students' understanding of the word *donate*? Imagine exploring it as follows:

TEACHER: We're being asked to donate food to the Food Bank. What does that mean, donate?

STUDENT: We give it to them.

TEACHER: So, *donate* means the same as *give*?

STUDENT: Give it to hungry people.

TEACHER: Can we ever talk about donating something other than food?

STUDENT: People donate blood

STUDENT: Or toys at Christmas.

TEACHER: So, how can you describe donate?

STUDENT: Give things away because someone else needs them.

The benefit of focusing on familiar words has been suggested by research into the depth of word knowledge. Studies have demonstrated (1) that people with more extensive vocabularies not only know more words but also know more about the words that they know (Curtis & Glaser, 1983), and (2) that people with high and lower vocabularies differ as to their depth of knowledge about even fairly common words (Van Daalen-Kapteijns & Elshout-Mohr, 1981).

What is gained from working with familiar words involves relationships among words, a topic we have visited before. Specifically, word knowledge exists not as a list of discrete items but as networks of words clustered into categories. For example, exploring that people donate different kinds of things, but in each case to fulfill a need, makes way for a new word—*recipient*—that students might never have thought about before. So, if that word is introduced, they have not only learned a new vocabulary item but have also developed a broader perspective on *donate*.

Along a similar line, it is also valuable to ask students to consider different uses for words that have likely been learned in particular contexts. For example, upper elementary school students may understand what an eclipse is (or may have even experienced one) when that word is encountered in a science text, or perhaps in news coverage of a current eclipse somewhere. But it would be useful to prompt students to think beyond the scientific event. For example: "You know that an eclipse happens when something like the moon comes between us and the sun, blocking the sun's light. So what do you think it would mean if, when we were watching a movie, I said, 'You're eclipsing my view of the screen'?" If students readily understand that usage, then their understanding can be moved a bit further. For example, "What would it mean to say that the performance of the chorus eclipsed that of the band?" It may take some interaction to help students realize that the latter example is no longer a physical "getting-in-the-way" meaning of *eclipse* but a metaphorical meaning of something overshadowing something else in importance or quality.

Another entry point for adding words to the environment is morphological relationships. For example, challenge students to compare *Tyrannosaurus* and *tyrant*; *pedestrian* and *pedal*; *duplicate* and *duplicity*. It can also be valuable to discuss when relationships seem to exist but do not, as in the case of *gargle* and *garden*. This can help students gain insight into language, such as the fact that the words we use come from many different sources including different languages, or sometimes simply imitate the sound of things, such as the word *gargle*. Including such ideas in discussions of words lets students see language as an open book rather than as mysterious and impenetrable with authority over them. Thus, explorations of words and word relationships can increase their motivation to find out about language, and use it confidently and playfully.

IN SUMMARY

This chapter has emphasized ways to create a lively verbal environment in classrooms. The teacher who is alert to opportunities for using sophisticated, interesting, and precise language is probably the most important element in such an environment. Teachers who revel in language are those who use words well and are eager to discover new words and word meanings. They play with words, rejoice in word lore, and model a genuine fascination for the feelings and images that words can evoke and create. In the classrooms of such teachers, there are books and posters and bulletin boards as well as conversations and contests that demonstrate a lively attention to words.

▪ *Your Turn* ▪

We invite you to use what you have learned in this chapter by selecting an activity from those listed below that interests you:

1. Select one of the books listed in Appendix B to review, and make a plan for sharing it with your students.
2. Select a poem with phrases that are particularly interesting or noteworthy and decide how you might share it with your students.
3. Find a group of words that share the same morpheme, or word root, and create a poster for several words that share it. For example, *tele*, meaning "far or distant," is the Greek word root for *telephone, television, telepathy,* and *telegraph.* Encourage students to create similar posters for other root words.

Text Talk Books and Vocabulary Words

KINDERGARTEN

Book/author	Publisher	Vocabulary words
Abiyoyo by Pete Seeger	Aladdin	*disappear* *precious* *foolish*
Annie and the Wild Animals by Jan Brett	Houghton Mifflin	*imagine* *snarl* *grumpy*
Biggest Nose by Kathy Caple	Houghton Mifflin	*continue* *measure* *commotion*
Brementown Musicians by Ilse Plume	Bantam Doubleday	*feast* *exhausted* *cautiously*
Can I Keep Him? by Steven Kellogg	Puffin Pied Piper	*annoy* *disagreeable* *appetite*
Caps for Sale by Esphyr Slobodkina	HarperCollins	*ordinary* *refreshed* *imitate*
Charlie Anderson by Barbara Abercrombie	Aladdin	*decide* *disappear* *prowl*

Book/author	Publisher	Vocabulary words
Cuddley Dudley by Jez Alborough	Candlewick Press	*disturb* *enormous* *resist*
Curious George Plays Baseball by Margret and H. A. Rey	Houghton Mifflin	*curious* *sneak* *hero*
Doctor DeSoto by William Steig	Farrar, Straus & Giroux	*timid* *morsel* *protect*
Friend for Growl Bear by Margot Austin	HarperCollins	*wise* *scowl* *peer*
Harriet by Deborah Inkpen	Barron's Educational Series	*gnaw* *horrible* *scurry*
Harry the Dirty Dog by Gene Zion	Harper Trophy	*except* *strange* *wonder*
Jessica Takes Charge by Linda LaRose	Annick Press	*soggy* *yelp* *nestle*
Little Bit of Winter by Paul Stewart	HarperCollins	*remind* *prod* *grasp*
Little Polar Bear and the Brave Little Hare by Hans de Beer	North South Books	*lean* *warn* *embarrassed*
Louie's Search by Ezra Jack Keats	Aladdin	*bellow* *gasp* *mumble*
Make Way for Ducklings by Robert McCloskey	Puffin Books	*enormous* *delighted* *beckoned*
Mop Top by Don Freeman	Puffin Books	*soaring* *vacant* *opposite*
Mouse in the House by Patricia Baehr	Holiday House	*toppled* *nibble* *appear*

Book/author	Publisher	Vocabulary words
Mrs. Potter's Pig by Phyllis Root	Candlewick Press	*glisten* *complain* *clutch*
Owen by Kevin Henkes	Green Willow	*essential* *absolutely* *perfect*
The Popcorn Dragon by Jane Thayer	Morrow Junior	*envious* *forlorn* *delighted*
Pretzel by Margret Rey	Houghton Mifflin	*distinguished* *appear* *admire*
Rusty Trusty Tractor by Joy Cowley	Boyds Mills Press	*regret* *sprout* *partial*
Sheila Rae, the Brave by Kevin Henkes	Mulberry Books	*fearless* *convince* *dashed*
Spike's Best Nest by Tony Maddox	Piccadilly Press	*grumpy* *delighted* *gloomy*

FIRST GRADE

Book/author	Publisher	Vocabulary words
Alexander and the Wind-Up Mouse by Leo Lionni	Knopf	*adventure* *searched* *envy*
Amos and Boris by William Steig	Farrar, Straus & Giroux	*miserable* *immense* *leisurely*
Beware of the Bears by Alan MacDonald	Little Tiger Press	*launched* *gleeful* *astonished*
Brave Irene by William Steig	Farrar, Straus & Giroux	*insisted* *coaxed* *cherish*

Book/author	Publisher	Vocabulary words
Curious George Takes a Job by H. A. Rey	Houghton Mifflin	*curious* *cozy* *mischief*
Edward the Emu by Sheena Knowles	HarperCollins	*amusing* *detest* *impressive*
Extraordinary Egg by Leo Lionni	Knopf	*impress* *triumphant* *extraordinary*
Giant Jam Sandwich by John Vernon Lord	Houghton Mifflin	*nuisance* *suggestion* *clever*
Harry and the Lady Next Door by Gene Zion	HarperCollins	*lovely* *contest* *shriek*
Hoppy and Joe by Betty Paraskevas	Simon & Schuster	*devotion* *weary* *persistent*
How Many Stars in the Sky? by Lenny Hort	Mulberry Books	*gazing* *dazzling* *instead*
Jamela's Dress by Niki Daly	Farrar, Straus & Giroux	*clutching* *cross* *radiant*
Metropolitan Cow by Tim Egan	Sandpiper	*fortunate* *dignified* *rambunctious*
Mole's Hill by Lois Ehlert	Harcourt Brace	*snarl* *quiver* *stroll*
Mr. Tanen's Ties by Maryann Cocca-Leffler	Whitman	*appropriate* *concentrate* *charming*
The Mysterious Tadpole by Steven Kellogg	Puffin Pied Piper	*mysterious* *eager* *ordinary*
Once a Mouse by Marcia Brown	Aladdin	*hermit* *comforted* *humble*

Book/author	Publisher	Vocabulary words
A Pocket For Corduroy by Don Freeman	Puffin Books	*insisted* *reluctant* *drowsy*
Possum's Harvest Moon by Anne Hunter	Houghton Mifflin	*autumn* *gaze* *creature*
Santa's Book of Names by David McPhail	Little, Brown	*patience* *lunge*
Shortest Kid in the World by Corinne Demas Bliss	Random House	*slump* *prefer* *announce*
Six-Dinner Sid by Inga Moore	Aladdin	*perfect* *suspicious*
Stephanie's Ponytail by Robert Munsch	Annick Press	*strange* *definitely* *bunch*
Sweet Strawberries by Phyllis Reynolds Naylor	Antheneum	*impatient* *stingy* *remarkable*
The Mitten by Jan Brett	Putnam	*commotion* *investigate* *admire*
Trouble on the T-Ball Team by Eve Bunting	Clarion Books	*mysterious* *trust* *shocked*
The Wolf's Chicken Stew by Keiko Kasza	Putnam & Grosset	*craving* *critters* *scrumptious*

SECOND GRADE

Book/author	Publisher	Vocabulary words
Beetle Boy by Lawrence David	Bantam Doubleday	*avoid* *hoist* *inspect*
Biggest Bear by Lynd Ward	Houghton Mifflin	*biggest* *chores* *especially*

Book/author	Publisher	Vocabulary words
Boy in the Drawer by Robert Munsch	Annick Press	*yank* *bother* *entirely*
The Bravest Dog Ever: The True Story of Balto by Natalie Standiford	Random House	*rescue* *arrive* *panic*
Burnt Toast on Davenport Street by Tim Egan	Houghton Mifflin	*familiar* *festive* *absurd*
Chestnut Cove by Tim Egan	Houghton Mifflin	*incredible* *ridiculous* *emotion*
The Cow Who Wouldn't Come Down by Paul Brett Johnson	Orchard Books	*sternly* *contrary* *ignored* *crouched*
Curious George Goes to a Chocolate Factory by Margret and H. A. Rey	Houghton Mifflin	*tour* *balcony* *search*
Dear Dr. Sillybear by Dian Curtis Regan	Holt	*examine* *advice* *splendid*
"Eat Your Vegetables" (from *Rats on the Roof*) by James Marshall	Puffin Books	*prefer* *ferocious* *budge*
Friday Night at Hodges' Café by Tim Egan	Houghton Mifflin	*satisfy* *menacing* *exquisite*
Grandpa's Teeth by Rod Clement	HarperCollins	*description* *complain* *suspect*
Ida and the Wool Smugglers by Sue Ann Alderson	Grandwood	*reply* *disappointed* *meadow*
Little House by Virginia Lee Burton	Houghton Mifflin	*notice* *shabby* *glance*
Little Island by Golden MacDonald	Bantam Doubleday	*faith* *prowl* *surrounded*

Book/author	Publisher	Vocabulary words
Livingstone Mouse by Pamela Duncan Edwards	HarperCollins	*murmur* *argumentative* *throbbed*
Mike Mulligan and the Steam Shovel by Virginia Lee Burton	Houghton Mifflin	*skyscraper* *cellar*
The Mountain That Loved a Bird by Alice McLerran	Simon & Schuster	*amazed* *nestle* *distance*
Nothing by Mick Inkpen	Orchard Books	*struggle* *reflection* *faded*
Patchwork Quilt by Valerie Flournoy	Dial Books	*masterpiece* *miserable* *dread*
Picnic at Mudsock Meadow by Patricia Polacco	Paperstar	*admit* *eerie* *vanished*
"Sheepish Tale" (from *Rats on the Roof*) by James Marshall	Puffin Books	*sensible* *pounce* *raucous*
Signmaker's Assistant by Tedd Arnold	Puffin Pied Piper	*wisdom* *informed* *realize*
Socrates by Rascal and Gert Bogarrts	Chronicle Books	*rummage* *squint* *deserves*
Space Case by Edward Marshall	Puffin Pied Piper	*uncooperative* *communicate* *peculiar*
Wolf by Becky Bloom	Orchard Books	*emergency* *concentrate* *impressed*

Books for a Lively Verbal Environment

LANGUAGE FOCUS

In *The Phantom Tollbooth* by Norton Juster (Random House, 1964), Milo discovers a world where words and phrases are more than just marks on a page. With the Spelling Bee, the watchdog Tock, and the Humbug, Milo meets King Azaz the Unabridged and his advisers, the Duke of Definition, the Minister of Meaning, the Earl of Essence, the Count of Connotation, and the Undersecretary of Understanding. In Dictionopolis, they feast on square meals and synonym buns before embarking on a journey through the Lands Beyond.

The Newbery award winner *The Westing Game* by Ellen Raskin (Puffin, 1992) is a mystery that compels readers to pay attention to words as clues in a memorable race to discover who Samuel W. Westing really is and who will inherit his fortune.

WORD HISTORIES

Some books that focus on the origin of words include the following:

- *A Chartreuse Leotard in a Magenta Limousine and Other Words Named after People and Places* by Lynda Graham-Barber (Hyperion, Newberry)
- *Dictionary of Word Origins: A History of the Words, Expressions and Cliches We Use* by J. Agee (Carol, 1995)

- *Guppies in Tuxedos and Other Funny Eponyms* by M. Terban (Clarion, 1988)
- *Merriam-Webster's New Book of Word Histories* (Merriam-Webster, 1991)
- *Where in the Word?: Extraordinary Stories Behind 801 Ordinary Words* by D. Muschell (Prima, 1990)

D'Aulaires' Book of Greek Myths by Ingri and Edgar Parin D'Aulaire (Doubleday, 1992) can prompt the study of names from Greek and Roman myths that were the origin for words we use today, such as *muses, museum; titans, titanic; Aphrodite, aphrodisiac; Pan, panic.*

MULTIPLE-MEANING WORDS

Students can discover the humor of multiple-meaning words, idioms, and homonyms (words that share the same spelling or pronunciation but differ in meaning and origin) in the Amelia Bedelia books by Peggy Parish such as *Teach Us, Amelia Bedelia* (Scholastic, 1977), and books by Fred Gwynne such as *The King Who Rained* (Simon & Schuster, 1970), *A Little Pigeon Toad* (Simon & Schuster, 1988), and *A Chocolate Moose for Dinner* (Aladdin, 1976).

KINDS OF WORDS

The New Reading Teacher's Book of Lists by E. B. Fry, D. L. Fountoukidis, and J. K. Polk (Prentice-Hall, 1985) is an excellent source for the following:

- Homophones, homographs
- Synonyms
- Antonyms
- Clipped words (e.g., *ad* for *advertisement*)
- Portmanteau words, or words that have been blended together (e.g., *modem* for *modulator* and *demodulator*)
- Compound words
- Acronyms, or words formed from initials (e.g., *ASAP* for *as soon as possible*)
- Onomatopoeia, or words that represent sounds (e.g., *clink*)

- Foreign words and phrases
- Greek and Latin roots
- Idioms

FANTASIES ABOUT WORDS

In the picture book *Alphabet Soup* by Kate Banks (Dragonfly Books, 1988), a young boy spells words in his soup, which causes the animals and people and objects he spells to appear.

For older readers, *Word Wizard* by Cathryn Falwell (Houghton Mifflin, 1998) describes a young girl who discovers that she can rearrange the letters in her alphabet cereal and make one thing turn into another. For example, she changes ocean into canoe to save herself and a boy who are in danger of being swept away. The book explains what anagrams are and encourages readers to create their own.

Two books about devouring rather than creating words are *The Word Eater* by Mary Amato (Holiday House, 2000) and *The Ink Drinker* by Eric Sanvoisin (Delacorte, 1998). The Word Eater is a worm named Fip who eats a word and makes whatever the word refers to disappear. The Ink Drinker is a mysterious fellow who lurks in a bookstore and uses a straw to drink the words out of books.

References

Ames, W. S. (1966/1967). The development of a classification scheme of contextual aids. *Reading Research Quarterly, 2,* 57–62.

Artley, A. S. (1943). Teaching word-meaning through context. *Elementary English Review, 20,* 68–74.

Banks, J. A., Beyer, B. K., Contreras, G., Craven, J., Ladson-Billings, G., McFarland, M. A., & Parker, S. C. (1997). *World: Adventures in time and place.* New York: Macmillan/McGraw-Hill.

Beck, I. L., & McKeown, M. G. (1985). Teaching vocabulary: Making the instruction fit the goal. *Educational Perspectives, 23*(1), 11–15.

Beck, I. L., & McKeown, M. G. (2001). Text Talk: Capturing the benefits of read-aloud experiences for young children. *The Reading Teacher, 55*(1), 10–20.

Beck, I. L., McKeown, M. G., & McCaslin, E. S. (1983). Vocabulary development: All contexts are not created equal. *The Elementary School Journal, 83*(3), 177–181.

Beck, I. L., McKeown, M. G., & Omanson, R. C. (1987). The effects and uses of diverse vocabulary instructional techniques. In M. G. McKeown & M. E. Curtis (Eds.), *The nature of vocabulary acquisition* (pp. 147–163). Hillsdale, NJ: Erlbaum.

Beck, I. L., Perfetti, C. A., & McKeown, M. G. (1982). Effects of long-term vocabulary instruction on lexical access and reading comprehension. *Journal of Educational Psychology, 74*(4), 506–521.

Biemiller, A. (1999). *Estimating vocabulary growth for ESL children with and without listening comprehension instruction.* Paper presented at the annual conference of the American Educational Research Association, Montréal, Québec, Canada.

Biemiller, A. (2001). Teaching vocabulary: Early, direct, and sequential. *The American Educator, 25*(1), 24–28.

Brontë, E. (1961). *Wuthering Heights.* New York: Scholastic. (Original work published 1847)

Calfee, R. C., & Drum, P. A. (1986). Research on teaching reading. In M. C. Wittrock (Ed.), *Handbook of research on teaching* (3rd ed., pp. 804–849). New York: Macmillan.

Carey, S. (1978). The child as word learner. In M. Halle, J. Bresnan, & G. Miller (Eds.), *Linguistic theory and psychological reality* (pp. 264–293). Cambridge, MA: MIT Press.

Christie, A. (1934). In a glass darkly. In L. Mountain, S. Crawley, & E. Fry (Eds.), *Jamestown Heritage Readers* (Book H, pp. 160–167). Providence, RI: Jamestown Publishers.

Collins COBUILD English language dictionary. (1987). London: Collins.

Cronbach, L. J. (1942). An analysis of techniques for diagnostic vocabulary testing. *Journal of Educational Research, 36, 206–217.*

Curtis, M. E. (1981). *Word knowledge and verbal aptitude.* Unpublished manuscript.

Curtis, M. E. (1987). Vocabulary testing and instruction. In M. G. McKeown & M. E. Curtis (Eds.), *The nature of vocabulary acquisition* (pp. 37–51). Hillsdale, NJ: Erlbaum.

Curtis, M. E., & Glaser, R. (1983). Reading theory and the assessment of reading achievement. *Journal of Educational Measurement, 20, 133–147.*

Cushman, K. (1994). *Catherine, called Birdy.* New York: Harper Trophy.

Dahl, R. (1972). *Charlie and the great glass elevator.* New York: Penguin.

Dale, E. (1965). Vocabulary measurement: Techniques and major findings. *Elementary English, 42, 82–88.*

Edwards, A. (2001). My father, the entomologist. *Cricket, 28*(10), 5–9.

Egan, T. (1995). *Chestnut Cove.* Boston: Houghton Mifflin.

Fleischman, P. (1988). Fireflies. In *Joyful noise: Poems for two voices.* New York: Harper Trophy.

Freeman, D. (1978). *A pocket for Corduroy.* New York: Puffin Books.

Goerss, B. L., Beck, I. L., & McKeown, M. G. (1999). Increasing remedial students' ability to derive word meaning from context. *Reading Psychology, 20*(2), *151–175.*

Graves, M. F. (1980, April). *A quantitative and qualitative study of students reading vocabularies.* Paper presented at the annual meeting of the American Education Research Association, Boston.

Graves, M. F., & Slater, W. H. (1987). *The development of reading vocabularies in rural disadvantaged students, inner-city disadvantaged students, and mid-*

dle-class suburban students. Paper presented at the meeting of the American Educational Research Association, Washington, DC.

Graves, M. F., Brunetti, G. J., & Slater, W. H. (1982). The reading vocabularies of primary-grade children of varying geographic and social backgrounds. In J. A. Harris & L. A. Harris (Eds.), *New inquiries in reading research and instruction* (pp. 99–104). Rochester, NY: National Reading Conference.

Hanks, P. (1987). Definitions and explanations. In J. M. Sinclair (Ed.), *Looking up* (pp. 116–136). London: Collins.

Hart, B., & Risley, T. (1995). *Meaningful differences.* Baltimore: Brookes. Co.

Joos, M. (1964). Language and the school child. *Harvard Educational Review, 34*, 203–210.

Juster, N. (1964). *The phantom tollbooth.* New York: Random House.

Kameenui, E. J., Dixon, D. W., & Carnine, R. C. (1987). Issues in the design of vocabulary instruction. In M. G. McKeown & M. E. Curtis (Eds.), *The nature of vocabulary acquisition* (pp. 129–145). Hillsdale, NJ: Erlbaum.

Kasza, K. (1987). *The wolf's chicken stew.* New York: Putnam & Grosset.

Kohnke, J. M. (2001). The pooka of Allihies. *Cricket, 28*(7), *12–16.*

Kucan, L., & Beck, I. L., (1996). Four fourth graders thinking aloud: An investigation of genre effects. *Journal of Literacy Research, 28*(2), *pp. 259–287.*

Landau, S. I. (1984). *Dictionaries: The art and craft of lexicography.* New York: Scribner.

MacDonald, A. (1999). *Beware of the bears.* Waukesha, WI: Little Tiger Press.

McCullough, C. M. (1943). Learning to use context clues. *Elementary English Review, 20, 140–143.*

McCullough, C. M. (1958). Context aids in reading. *Reading Teacher, 11, 224–229.*

McKeown, M. G. (1985). The acquisition of word meaning from context by children of high and low ability. *Reading Research Quarterly, 20*(4), *482–496.*

McKeown, M. G. (1991). Learning word meanings from definitions: Problems and potential. In P. Schwanenflugel (Ed.), *The psychology of word meanings* (pp. 137–156). Hillsdale, NJ: Erlbaum.

McKeown, M. G. (1993). Creating effective definitions for young word learners. *Reading Research Quarterly, 28, 16–31.*

McKeown, M. G., & Beck, I. L. (in press). Taking advantage of read alouds to help children make sense of decontextualized language. In A. van Kleeck, S. A. Stahl, & E. B. Bauer (Eds.), *Storybook reading.* Mahwah, NJ: Erlbaum.

McKeown, M. G., Beck, I. L., Omanson, R. C., & Perfetti, C. A. (1983). The effects of long-term vocabulary instruction on reading comprehension: A replication. *Journal of Reading Behavior, 15*(1), *3–18.*

McKeown, M. G., Beck, I. L., Omanson, R. C., & Pople, M. T. (1985). Some effects of the nature and frequency of vocabulary instruction on the knowledge and use of words. *Reading Research Quarterly, 20*(5), 522–535.

Miller, G. A. (1978). Semantic relations among words. In M. Halle, J. Bresnan, & G. A. Miller (Eds.), *Linguistic theory and psychological reality* (pp. 61–118). Cambridge, MA: MIT Press.

Miller, G. A. & Gildea, P. M. (1985). How to misread a dictionary. *AILA Bulletin*. Pisa, Italy: International Association for Applied Linguistics.

Moore, I. (1991). *Six-dinner Sid*. New York: Aladdin.

Nagy, W. E., & Anderson, R. C. (1984). How many words are there in printed school English? *Reading Research Quarterly, 19, 304–330*.

Nagy, W. E., Herman, P., & Anderson, R. (1985). Learning words from context. *Reading Research Quarterly, 20, 233–253*.

Nagy, W. E., & Scott, J. A. (2000). Vocabulary processes. In M. L. Kamil, P. B. Mosenthal, P., David Pearson, & R. Barr (Eds.), *Handbook of reading research* (Vol. III, pp. 69–284). Mahwah, NJ: Erlbaum.

Rankin, E. F., & Overholser, B. M. (1969). Reaction of intermediate-grade children to contextual clues. *Journal of Reading Behavior, 1, 50–73*.

Rey, M., & Rey, H. A. (1998). *Curious George goes to a chocolate factory*. Boston: Houghton Mifflin.

Scott, J. A., & Nagy, W. E. (1989, December). *Fourth graders' knowledge of definitions and how they work*. Paper presented at the annual meeting of the National Reading Conference, Austin, TX.

Scott, J. A., Jamieson, D., & Asselin, M. (1998). *Learning words: Findings from 69 days in 23 intermediate classrooms*. Paper presented at the annual meeting of the American Educational Research Association, San Diego, CA.

Smith, M. K. (1941). Measurement of the size of general English vocabulary through the elementary grades and high school. *Genetic Psychological Monographs, 24, 311–345*.

Stahl, S. A., & Fairbanks, M. M. (1986). The effects of vocabulary instruction: A model-based meta-analysis. *Review of Educational Research, 56, 72–110*.

Steig, W. (1982). *Doctor DeSoto*. New York: Farrar, Straus & Giroux.

Swanborn, M. S. L., & de Glopper, K. (1999). Incidental word learning while reading: A meta-analysis. *Review of Educational Researach, 69*(3), pp. 261–285.

Taylor, M. D. (1976). *Roll of thunder, hear my cry*. New York: Penguin.

Thayer, J. (1953). *The popcorn dragon*. New York: Morrow.

Twain, M. (1992). *The prince and the pauper*. New York: Penguin. (Original work published 1881)

Van Daalen-Kapteijns, M. M., & Elshout-Mohr, M. (1981). The acquisition of word meanings as a cognitive learning process. *Journal of Verbal Learning and Verbal Behavior, 20,* 386–399.

Watts, S. M. (1995). Vocabulary instruction during reading lessons in six classrooms. *Journal of Reading Behavior, 27,* 399–424.

Werner, H., & Kaplan, E. (1952). The acquisition of word meaning: A developmental study. *Monographs of the Society of Research in Child Development, 15*(1, Serial No. 51).

White, E. B. (1952). *Charlotte's web.* New York: Harper & Row.

Index